Bread
& Baking

Author: Annette Wolter
Photography: Rolf Feuz and Karin Messerli
Translated by UPS Translations, London
Edited by Josephine Bacon

CLB 4272
This edition published in 1995 by Colour Library Books Ltd
Published originally under the title "Brot und Herzhaftes Gebäck"
by Gräfe und Unzer Verlag GmbH, München
© 1995 Gräfe und Unzer Verlag GmbH, München
English translation copyright: © 1995 by
Colour Library Books Ltd, Godalming, Surrey
Typeset by Image Setting, Brighton, E. Sussex
Printed and bound in Singapore
All rights reserved
ISBN 1-85833-319-9

BREAD
& BAKING

Annette Wolter

Contributors
Cornelia Adam, Elke Alsen,
Dagmar von Cramm, Marey Kurz,
Hannelore Mähl-Strenge, Annedore Meineke,
Bernd Schiansky, Brigitta Stuber

Photography
Rolf Feuz and Karin Messerli

CLB
Colour Library Books

Contents

Snacks and Savouries

Essential Ingredients for Baking

Baking Tins and Kitchen Equipment

Pizzas, Flans and quiches

Index

About this Book

Baking has a good deal to do with anticipation. People bake for holidays, special occasions, as a treat for favourite guests and to celebrate birthdays. These days, many people have transferred their culinary allegiance from sweet to savoury. They now appreciate the appeal of thickly-topped pizzas, seafood quiches, tender vegetable flans with creamy fillings, delicate cheese pastries and tangy tartlets just as much as they once enjoyed thickly-iced birthday cakes and elaborate gateaux for special occasions. Home-made bread and crusty rolls have also found their way into the repertoires of many enthusiastic cooks who bake in their spare time.

This illustrated cookery book includes recipes for many different types of savoury baking. The colour photographs, commissioned especially for this book, show you the tempting results baking can produce, and help you to make the right choice of recipe, whether you are looking for something special for a dinner party, or a suitable addition to the picnic hamper or the Sunday breakfast table.

We have worked very hard to select a broad range of recipes. The authors put their long years of experience and cooking skills into creating the variety of recipes in the individual chapters. The result consists of many popular and well-known breads and rolls, tempting snacks and traditional and newly-invented savoury breads and pastries.

Each chapter offers a selection of particularly nutritious recipes. There are also breads baked in traditional style, using flour from the wide variety of grains that are becoming increasingly available through health food shops. Many of the breads are baked with wholegrain flour. Remember, a wholegrain flour dough is always a little stickier than a dough made from refined flour. In the opening pages of the book you will find information and step-by-step photographs on preparing bread dough as well as tips on handling yeast, sourdough, starter and baking powder. You will be shown how to shape fancy breads and rolls. There are also hints on toppings and fillings for pizzas, flans and other savoury pastries.

All the recipes have been thoroughly tested and you will find that they are explained in a simple, easy-to-follow language, to guarantee success. There are helpful tips indicating variations on the basic theme of the bread in question. Particularly nutritious recipes and classic recipes are also highlighted. The information provided on preparation, baking and assembly times allows you to plan your baking sensibly. Each recipe is accompanied by a nutritional analysis, indicating the energy content in kJoules and kcalories, and the protein, fat and carbohydrate content. This is important for meal-planning and for people for whom a healthy diet is important.

There are four main chapters. The first, Fragrant Breads, offers a wide variety of breads, from simple breakfast table breads to loaves flavoured with exotic spices, and ethnic breads. The Rolls and Creative Baking chapter demonstrates how varied and delicious rolls and pastries can be, and includes recipes for Buckwheat Rolls, Catherine Wheels, Muffins, Herbed Scones, Pretzels, Plaited Loaves, Croissants and Ring Rolls. The third chapter, Snacks and Savouries, offers nibbles for all kinds of occasions. These include Cheese Biscuits, Beer Sticks and Grissini, Turnovers, and pasties and tartlets with delicious fillings. The final chapter, Pizzas and Quiches, features a whole range of popular pizzas, tasty pies, delicious tarts and tempting quiches which are a little out-of-the-ordinary and perfectly suited to informal entertaining.

The essential ingredients required for baking are described and pictured at the back of the book, after the recipe chapters. The diffrence is explained between refined and wholegrain flours. The properties of the various raising agents are discussed and further tips are given on how to use spices in your baking and how to combine doughs. You will also find a guide to the best baking tins, and hints on the kind of kitchen equipment which will make baking easier and more likely to succeed.

There is an extensive index to help you to find the recipe you require. Unless, of course, you simply allow yourself to browse through the book, inspired by the brilliant colour photographs which give you a visual foretaste of how the recipe will turn out and tempt you to try it.

(The kJ and kcal abbreviations in the recipes stand for kiloJoule and kilocalories.)

Practical Tips

Why bake your own bread?

The variety of bread and rolls currently available in the shops is greater than ever. Nevertheless, buying wholegrain bread remains a matter of trust if you feel strongly about wholegrain bread. According to the Trades Descriptions Act, wheatmeal bread and rolls must contain at least 30 per cent wholegrain flour. However, sometimes all this means is that a handful of grains has been kneaded into the dough. Some big bakers even colour their brown breads with caramel, to make them look like a wholemeal product. Many people believe that yeast baking is difficult – in fact, it is much easier than you might think. We have put together these important practical tips so that even your first home-baked bread will be a success.

The first steps

The dough must be allowed to rise in peace for the baked result to be sufficiently light and tasty. Warmth is the main requirement for this. The ingredients for the dough, which should be measured accurately, must not come straight from the refrigerator, and the kitchen should be at normal room temperature (about 22°C/70°F). Sudden draughts are also a menace. When leaving a dough to rise the way to judge when it is ready is to see the amount by which the dough has actually increased in bulk rather than the time stated in the recipe. If a sourdough is supposed to take 12 hours to rise at a room temperature of 22°C/70°F but this temperature cannot be guaranteed, leave the dough in the oven with the pilot light switched on or in an airing cupboard, both of which will produce a temperature of around 24°C/75°F. A yeast dough is only occasionally refrigerated, for example, for yeast puff dough, to make it more pliable and easier to work, or to retard the rising so that dough made at night can be baked in the morning.

Thorough kneading is required to give the bread a light texture. Kneading dough by hand is still the best way of ensuring the dough is just right, but it is easier and faster to use the dough hook on an electric mixer or the blades of a food processor. Make sure the blades are not too cold.

Proving the dough

Yeast dough lends itself well to being shaped by hand after it has been allowed to rise for the first time. The second rising, which takes place after the bread has been shaped, is called proving. If you leave bread to prove for too long it may spread out over the whole baking sheet during baking. On the other hand, too little proving time makes the end-product heavy. Dough made from wholewheat flour or using a sourdough starter should be wetter than other types of dough, although if the consistency is too liquid you may end up with a large, flat, pancake-like bread. However, a bread dough should be fairly moist; if the dough is too stiff, the bread will probably turn out too dry.

Baking temperatures and times

In these recipes, baking temperatures are given in degrees Fahrenheit and Celsius. You should test the heat of your own oven, as many vary in efficiency, and consult the manufacturer's handbook. An oven thermometer will establish the accuracy of your oven. Depending on the type of oven, it will be necessary to preheat it for 10 or 15 minutes before you wish to start baking, in order for it to reach the required temperature. This takes only a few minutes with a gas oven, but fan-assisted and modern electric ovens need almost no pre-heating at all. Although you should use slightly lower temperatures if you have a fan-assisted oven, stick to the same baking times.

Before placing the bread in the oven, put a cup of water on the oven floor, so that the bread gets enough steam.

Handling freshly baked bread

The first step is to test whether the bread is done. Turn the hot bread out on to a cloth and tap the underside. If it sounds hollow, it is done. Wholegrain bread should be sprayed or brushed with cold water as soon as it is removed from the oven, so that the crust does not harden, and to make it easier to slice. This also gives the bread a nice golden-brown colour. In the past, bakers used a thick, compact brush for this. Nowadays a plant-sprayer or a sturdy pastry brush does the job perfectly. Wholegrain bread and bread made from mixed grain flours should be left for 12 to 24 hours after baking, so that it slices easily. White bread is at its best straight from the oven.

Storing and freezing bread

Rye breads stay fresh longer than wheaten breads. White bread which is a few days old can be sliced and toasted, or slowly baked into rusks; rolls can be sprayed with water and heated in the oven.

Bread should be stored in a cool, well-ventilated place. It should never be kept in plastic bags as this causes mould to form.

There is no loss of nutritional value or taste when bread is frozen. Savoury pastries and rolls can also be frozen and, once reheated in the oven, they taste as if they were freshly baked.

Oven Temperatures		
°C	°F	Gas Mark
110	225	1/4
150	300	2
180	350	4
200	400	6
230	450	8

Different Types of Starter and Dough

Yeast starter

Breads made from yeast doughs are often light breads containing refined or mixed grain flours. Yeast dough must be allowed to rise twice and prove once to prevent the crumb from becoming too soft and aerated. You should plan the timing of your bread baking carefully, as yeast breads taste best when freshly made (however, yeast bread can be frozen fresh from the oven and any leftover slices toasted). If you are working with fresh yeast or active dry yeast, which are both good sources of the vitamin B complex, you first have to make a starter or leaven. This procedure is not necessary if you are using the type of dried yeast that can be mixed directly with the dry ingredients. All the ingredients for the dough must be at room temperature but no hotter than blood heat. Try and ensure that the kitchen is as dry as possible. Even the weather outside makes a difference; bread will rise better on a sunny day than on a wet one.

One way a making the yeast starter or leaven, which is widely used on the Continent, is to weigh all the flour used in the recipe and sift it into a large bowl. Make a well in the centre. Crumble fresh yeast into the well and sprinkle with a teaspoon of sugar. Add 100 ml/4 fl oz of the liquid used in the recipe and mix in a little of the flour.

Kneading the yeast dough

In general, the longer and more thoroughly a yeast dough is kneaded, the lighter the bread, although it can be overkneaded. You should never knead for longer than 20 minutes. The gluten present in wheat is essential for this process as it makes the dough light and elastic. The yeast gives off carbon dioxide, causing a considerable increase in the volume of the dough. Flours such as rye and barley have a much lower gluten content, and cornmeal has no gluten at all. Rye is often mixed with wheat to make rye bread that is lighter and rises more quickly. The other flours must be mixed with wheat to make a yeast-risen bread or, as in the case or cornbread, they are risen with baking powder and sour milk or buttermilk. Kneading a heavy dough by hand is time-consuming and hard work. If you find it too strenuous, use a food processor, or a mixer with a dough hook, though hand-kneading is best.

If other ingredients are to be added, these must also be at room temperature. Add them at the edge of the bowl. Add the remaining lukewarm liquid and mix it in, either with the dough hook of an electric hand mixer, or with a wooden spoon.

Using baking powder as a raising agent

Bread made with baking powder is made rather like sourdough bread. It is a fairly simple process, but takes time. Baking powder is particularly useful as a raising agent for breads made from grains such as rye, oats and barley, which are low or lacking in gluten. The dough rises mainly because of the effect of warmth during long standing periods rather than due to intensive kneading. In summer, leave the dough to rise in a warm, shady place; in winter use the oven, with the pilot light or interior light switched on, maintaining a constant temperature of 24°C/75°F to 28°C/82°F. Like sourdough bread, bread made with baking powder should not be sliced until one day after baking. If it is stored in a cool, dry place, it will stay fresh for up to 14 days.

Combine 250g/8oz freshly ground wholemeal rye flour in a bowl with 1 tsp baking powder, 1 tsp tartaric acid, 500ml/18 fl oz lukewarm water and 2 tbsps liquid honey. Cover and leave to rise in a warm place for 24 hours at 24°C /75°F (min.). The surface should then be light and foaming.

Making your own sourdough

Sourdough bread is usually made from rye or a mixture of wholegrain flours. It has a slightly sour taste and stays fresh for a long time. Healthfood shops stock sourdough starter. To make your own natural sourdough, use sourdough extract or liquid sourdough as a starter. With time and patience, however, you can even make your own sourdough from wheat or rye flour. Although making a sourdough is time-consuming, it can be used over and over. After making the first batch of bread, keep back some of the dough and refrigerate it (it will keep for up to six months). Use it as the basis for the next batch of sourdough bread. In this way, you can go on making sourdough breads indefinitely from one original sourdough fermentation.

On the first day, mix 200g/7oz finely ground wheat or rye flour with 250ml/9 fl oz lukewarm water and 2 to 3 tbsps buttermilk in a large, tall earthenware pot or crock. Cover with a damp cloth and leave to stand at a temperature of at least 24°C/75°F.

Alternatively, crumble the fresh yeast or pour the active dry yeast into a small bowl, add a teaspoon of sugar and about 100ml/4 fl oz of lukewarm liquid. Cover and stand for 15 minutes. If the mixture is frothy, the yeast is working and this starter can be mixed with the dry ingredients This is a very good way to ensure that your yeast is active; if the liquid does not froth, the yeast is not working and you will have to throw it away and start again.

Dust the dough with flour, cover with a damp cloth or clingfilm and leave to rise for 15 to 30 minutes in a warm, draught-free place at room temperature (approx. 22°C/70°F). Make sure there is plenty of room in the bowl for the dough to rise. The surface of the flour will now have fine cracks across it.

Now knead the dough by hand just until it leaves the bowl clean. Transfer the dough to a floured work surface and knead it thoroughly with the heel of your hand for about 10 minutes, folding and turning it slightly with each movement. By the end it should be elastic and springy.

Shape the dough into a ball and cover it with a damp cloth or clingfilm. Leave in a warm place until it has doubled in bulk – this should take between 45 minutes and one hour. Knead again and then mould into the shape required by the recipe or put into a loaf tin. The second rising that most breads need, after the dough has been shaped is called proving. The dough should be proved for at least 30 minutes. Some yeast dough recipes call for second and even third provings.

Into this starter, stir the same quantity of wholegrain flour and 250ml/9 fl oz lukewarm water. Cover and leave to rise for 12 more hours at 24°C/75°F (min.). Fermentation should be even more obvious by now: the foam will have subsided and the dough will have a yeasty smell.

Add about 700g/1lb 10oz mixed wholegrain flour and/or coarsely ground grains (depending on the recipe), salt and spices to the starter dough and knead to make an elastic, slightly sticky dough. Put the dough into the greased loaf tin and leave to rise for a further 2 hours or until it has increased in bulk by one third.

On the second day, stir in 100g/4oz wholemeal wheat or rye flour and 250ml/9 fl oz warm water. On the third day, add 100g/4oz wholemeal wheat or rye flour and 125ml/4 fl oz warm water. Keep the container at a constant, warm temperature and keep covered with a cloth.

On the fourth day, add a further 100g/4oz wholemeal wheat or rye flour and 125ml/4 fl oz warm water. Cover and leave to stand. During fermentation the sourdough should foam and rise each time.
If the sourdough is reddish in colour at this time or has not risen, it is no good and must be discarded.

Different Types of Starter and Dough

Starter from bread dough

You can make a starter again and again in a much less time-consuming process than the one just described if you put aside a little raw bread dough from one batch to use as a basis for making the next batch of dough. This works with both yeast-based and baking powder doughs. You can freeze the dough for up to 14 days. To defrost it, leave it for an hour in lukewarm water, press it down with a wooden spoon, leave for another hour and then beat with a whisk. Then use the method illustrated and described to make the starter dough in about 18 hours:

Place 200g/7oz raw dough in a large bowl and cover with 500ml/18 fl oz lukewarm water. Cover and leave to rise in a warm place (min. 24°C) for 30 minutes. Using a wooden spoon, cut the dough into pieces and leave for a further 30 minutes.

Savoury shortcrust pastry

Savoury shortcrust pastry is usually used for the sort of light dough crust required for a pie, tart or quiche, and for many other savoury pastries with cheese, vegetable and meat fillings. Unlike a yeast dough, the ingredients for shortcrust pastry must be cold and should be incorporated quickly. Once the dough has been kneaded, leave it in the refrigerator for 30 minutes to an hour. Shortcrust dough should be firm enough to be rolled out easily and made into the shapes required by the recipe. Shortcrust dough basically consists of flour, a pinch of salt and fat; adding 1 small egg or an egg yolk will stop the dough from becoming too crumbly.

Sift 250g/8oz flour on to a work surface, make a well in the centre and break the egg yolk into it. Cut 125g/5oz chilled butter into cubes and add to the flour with 2 tbsps ice-cold water and 1/2 tsp salt. Cut the ingredients together, using a dough scraper or a pastry cutter.

Bread dough with vegetables

Vegetables can enhance the taste, colour and texture of bread. Try using grated courgettes, beetroot or carrots, diced onions fried gently in butter, cooked and puréed pumpkin, tomato purée or steamed, mashed potatoes. The amount of water used in the basic bread recipe should be reduced as vegetables contain fluid, but otherwise the process of making the dough is the same. Cooked vegetables should be cooled slightly so that they are lukewarm when mixed in with the starter, seasoning and flour.

Knead the yeast mixture with wholewheat flour, salt, 250g/8oz grated courgettes, dried thyme and as much lukewarm buttermilk as required to form an elastic dough. Cover and leave to rise at room temperature for 1 hour.

Flatbreads

This special bread is made all over the world. Flatbreads come in squares, rounds and ovals, can be made of wheat or rye flour or a combination of the two, or even of other flours. They may be leavened or unleavened. If unleavened they may be baked immediately or left for the natural enzymes in flour to soften them. sprinkled with poppy seeds, sesame or caraway seeds or coarse salt, or simply dusted with flour. Some are cooked in a heavy pan or griddle on the hob, others are baked in the oven and a few on hot stones over an open fire. If they are baked for a long time they are wonderfully crisp; those baked for a shorter time are softer and thinner. When spread with garlic paste, herb butter or pâté they are delicious rolled or folded up.

Make a basic yeast bread dough with wholewheat flour. When it has proved, divide it into equal-sized pieces and, with floured hands, shape into balls. On a floured work surface roll these out into oval shapes 1cm/1/2in thick

Stir the dough and add 250g/8oz wholewheat flour. Leave in a warm place (at least 24℃/75℉) for 12 hours.

Stir in a further 250g/8oz wholewheat flour and 250ml/9 fl oz lukewarm water; cover and leave to rise for a further 6 hours. The sourdough is now ready for use.

Mix rapidly together to form an elastic dough. Shape into a ball and refrigerate for 30 minutes to an hour, either covered or wrapped in aluminium foil or clingfilm. In the meantime, prepare any filling required by the recipe.

Roll the pastry out on a lightly floured work surface and process according to the recipe. For example, you could make pasties by cutting the dough into 12x12cm/5x5in squares, spooning on the prepared filling on each square and folding the corners together to make a triangle. Brush with egg yolk and press the edges firmly.

Knead the dough again thoroughly and shape into an oval loaf. Place on an oiled baking sheet, cover and leave to rise for 30 minutes. Using a razor blade, make three diagonal incisions on the surface, brush with olive oil and bake on the centre shelf of the oven until golden-brown.

Test whether the bread is done by turning it out onto a cloth and tapping the underside. If it sounds hollow, it is done. Leave the courgette bread to cool on a wire rack before slicing.

Brush the flatbreads with melted butter, sprinkle with sesame seeds and place immediately on a heated, greased baking sheet. Bake on the centre shelf of a hot oven for 10 to 20 minutes, or cook under a hot grill, turning half-way through cooking, until lightly browned.

Serve warm with a topping of your choice. These breads are especially popular in the Middle East, where toppings include cooked, diced lamb, garlic, fresh coriander onion, red peppers and chillies, feta cheese puréed with olive oil and mixed with chopped mint and parsley.

Shaping the Bread

Making loaves

Crusty bread can be made into just about any shape you require. You can shape it by hand or simply bake it in a loaf tin, a cake tin or even a tall mould like a large coffee tin. Basket bread, a popular Continental product, has a groove-like pattern on its surface. This is achieved by shaping the dough into a round or oval, and then leaving it to prove in a floured bread-basket made of cane. The loaf is then slid on to the greased baking sheet to be baked. Bread can also be baked in a brick (an unglazed earthenware crock), in flowerpots, in a cast iron pan or a cake tin.

To make a farmhouse loaf, shape the risen dough into a ball with floured hands, flatten it slightly, cover and leave to rise for another 30 minutes. Before baking, brush the loaf with water or milk. Dip a sharp knife in water and use it to cut a chequered pattern on the surface.

Making plaited loaves

Plaited loaves always look attractive and in many cultures they are the classic bread for special occasions. If you have the time and patience, make 8 to 10 small plaits from the dough. You can then make a whole garland of plaits, starting with a single large plait and pressing the ends firmly together. The pictures show you how to produce a double plait – the finished product looks complicated, but it is actually quite straightforward to make.

Make a yeast dough using strong, plain white flour. Knead it and leave it to rise until doubled in bulk. Weigh the dough and divide it into 2 portions, one twice as heavy as the other.

Different sorts of rolls

Rolls have all sorts of different names, there are bridge rolls and kaiser rolls, sandwich and cloverleaf rolls, caraway and salt fingers. They usually consist of a yeast dough, made with milk, water or salt; sometimes eggs are added. If you want a golden-brown crust, brush the rolls prior to baking with lukewarm water, milk, beaten egg or egg yolk. Rolls made with refined flour, wholegrain flour and combined flours can be sprinkled with poppy seeds or sesame seeds, ground coriander, caraway, sunflower and pumpkin seeds, linseed, nigella or coarse salt, or a mixture of these. Rye rolls are good topped with chopped walnuts or freshly grated Cheddar cheese.

Divide the yeast dough into 50g/2oz pieces. With floured hands, shape the pieces into balls, place on a greased baking sheet, cover and leave to rise for 15 minutes. Brush with lukewarm water and dust with a little flour. Make one diagonal incision and leave to rise for a further 15 minutes.

Light brioches

This Parisian speciality has become well known outside France and Switzerland. Brioches, large and small, are now enjoyed at breakfast tables the world over. Brioches require a buttery yeast dough, which makes the finished product light and crumbly. You can buy special brioche tins but you can also use vol-au-vent cases; bright paper cases are ideal for mini-brioches as they can then be served as they are. For normal sized brioches you should proceed as follows:

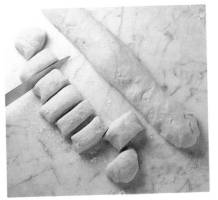

Make yeast dough from 500g/12oz flour, 30g/1oz yeast, 50g/2oz sugar, 125ml/4 fl oz lukewarm milk, 3 eggs, 200g/7oz soft butter and a generous pinch of salt. Roll it out on a floured work surface to form a long roll. Divide this into 20 pieces.

Alternatively, shape the dough into an oval loaf, brush it with beer, sprinkle with caraway seeds and make three or four incisions in the surface. Cover and leave to rise for 30 minutes. The earlier the incisions are made in the shaped bread, the more they will expand during baking.

Another method is to knead the dough again thoroughly after it has proved once, shape it into an oblong loaf and place in a greased loaf tin. Brush the surface with water, milk or beaten egg and, using a razor blade, make a cut $\frac{1}{2}$cm/$\frac{1}{4}$in cut all the way down the centre. Cover and leave to rise in the tin for 30 minutes.

Divide each portion into 3 pieces and roll by hand into sausage shapes on a floured work surface. Weave the sausages into plaits and press the ends together.

Set the smaller plait on the larger and press them gently together. Beat 1 egg yolk with 2 teaspoons water. Line the baking sheet with greaseproof or baking paper and place the plait on the tray. Brush it with egg yolk, cover and leave to rise. Brush with a little more egg yolk and bake until golden.

For caraway or salty fingers, roll out the risen and thoroughly kneaded dough to a thickness of 1cm/$\frac{1}{2}$in and a diameter of 25cm/10in. Cut diagonally into 4 or 8 pieces. Roll up the triangles from the base to the apex, leave to rise for 15 minutes, brush with beaten egg and sprinkle on caraway seeds or coarse salt.

To make cloverleaf rolls, divide the dough into 60g/2oz pieces and divide each of these into three. With wet hands, shape the pieces into balls and cluster them together in groups of three. Leave the cloverleaf rolls to rise for 15 minutes, then brush with a mixture of egg yolk and milk and sprinkle with poppy seeds or grated cheese.

Cut off one quarter of each piece of dough and, with floured hands, shape it into balls. Set the larger ball in the greased tins and make a small indentation in the top. Brush the indentation with beaten egg yolk and set the smaller ball on top.

Cover with a cloth and leave to rise in a warm place for 15 minutes. Bake on the centre shelf at 220°C/425°F/Gas Mark 7 for 15 to 20 minutes until golden-brown.

Handy Tips

Making fancy breads

You can make all sorts of fancy breads in interesting shapes using simple techniques.

1 Roll out the dough to a thickness of 1cm/½in and cut 25cm/10in long strips. Sprinkle some poppy seeds over the work surface and roll the dough strips up from both ends to meet in the middle.

2 Roll out fingers of dough 25cm/10in long and 2cm/1in thick. Roll each end round into a pinwheel shape in a different direction, until they meet in the middle.

3 Roll up the ends of the dough fingers to form small twists and put one twist on top of another.

4 Roll out 40cm/16in long, thin fingers of dough, leaving the ends a little fatter than the middles. Make a loop, fold each end down and roll it up.

Making creative shapes

A real surprise for your party guests, or an original gift.

1 Shape the dough into 18 equal-sized balls. On a floured work surface, roll 9 of the balls into 15cm/6in long fingers. Shape into rings.

2 Grease the baking sheet or line it with baking paper and place one dough ball in the centre.

3 Lay the rings all round the ball. Roll the other 9 balls into 18cm/7in long fingers and shape into crescents. Place them on the sheet, joining the rings together.

4 Sprinkle the centre roll and the two rows of rings and crescents with seeds of different colours, for instance, alternate sesame with poppy seed, or sesame with caraway and coarse salt.

Making pizza

This flatbread with topping whose popularity is now worldwide, is best made from a yeast dough. Pizzas are usually round, though they can also be baked in rectangular baking sheets.

1 For a Four Seasons Pizza, roll out a circle 20cm/8in in diameter, raising the dough up slightly at the edges. Lay the pizza on an oiled baking sheet and lightly mark out four quarters.

2 Arrange sliced tomatoes, mushrooms, ham, green pepper rings, artichokes and salami on the four quarters.

3 Season with salt, pepper and dried rosemary. Sprinkle with chopped anchovies and freshly grated Parmesan cheese.

4 Drizzle on 1 tbsp olive oil and bake on the centre shelf of the oven until crispy and golden.

Making quiches

These open pies from France use a thin shortcrust dough. The filling is usually based on a savoury custard mixture and can contain a wide variety of ingredients. This is an unusual version because it also has a top crust.

1 For a spinach quiche, roll out two-thirds of well-chilled shortcrust dough on a lightly floured work surface to form a 32cm/13in circle. Butter the bottom and sides of a springform tin. Lift the dough with a rolling pin and place it in the tin.

2 Cook the spinach until wilted, drain it thoroughly and let it cool. Spread half of it over the pastry base. Arrange halved hard-boiled eggs in a circle on top.

3 Cover with the remaining spinach. Beat two egg yolks with 250 ml/8 fl oz single cream and pour this over the spinach.

4 Use the rest of the dough to roll out a 26cm/11in circle. Using the floured rolling pin to help lift the other dough circle, place the lid on top of the filling and press the edges down firmly. Prick with a fork to ensure that the steam escapes evenly during baking.

Fragrant Bread

Some of these delicious breads are
time-consuming, but the result
is well worth the effort

Wheaten Loaves

A mixture of wholemeal and wheatmeal (partial extraction) flours, plus wheatgerm form the basis for this delicious breads

Hand-shaped Wheaten Bread
illustrated left

Quantities for 2 loaves:
1.5kg/3lbs organic wholemeal flour

1 tsp salt

84g/3oz fresh yeast or 42g/1½oz dry yeast

250g/8oz wheatmeal flour

1 tsp sugar

2 tbsps wheatgerm

500ml/18 fl oz lukewarm water

4 tbsps milk

Baking paper for the baking sheet

Preparation time: 30 minutes
Rising time: 1 hour 45 minutes
Baking time: 50 minutes
Nutritional value:
Analysis per slice, if 2 loaves divided into 50 slices, approx:
- 460kJ/110kcal
- 4g protein
- 1g fat
- 22g carbohydrate

Combine the wholemeal flour and salt in a bowl, cover and leave in a warm place. • Crumble the fresh yeast over the flour, mix with the sugar, a little water and the flour. If using dry yeast, blend with the sugar and water and pour this over the flour. Cover and leave to rise in a warm place for 30 minutes. • Knead the wheatmeal flour, wheatgerm and the remaining water into the yeast mixture. Knead the dough until smooth and elastic and then leave to rise in a warm place for 45 minutes. • Line the baking sheet with baking paper. • Knead the dough with floured hands. Shape it into two loaves. Place them on the baking sheet, cover and leave to prove for 30 minutes. • Place a dish of cold water on the oven floor. • Make four cuts across the tops of the loaves and brush with milk. Bake on the bottom shelf of a preheated 220°C/425°F/Gas Mark 7 oven for 50 minutes or until golden-brown.

Wheatmeal Loaf
illustrated right

Quantities for 1 30cm/12in loaf:
750g/1lb 11oz wholewheat flour

750g/1lb 11oz wheatmeal flour

2 tbsps wheatgerm

63g/2½oz fresh yeast or 32g/1oz dry yeast

500ml/18 fl oz lukewarm water

1 tsp salt

1 tbsp melted butter

Oil for the tin

Preparation time: 30 minutes
Rising time: 14 hours
Baking time: 50 minutes
Nutritional value:
Analysis per slice, if divided into 30 slices, approx:
- 670kJ/160kcal
- 6g protein
- 1g fat
- 31g carbohydrate

Combine the flours in a bowl, add the wheatgerm and make a well in the centre. Crumble the fresh yeast into the well. Add 400ml/14 fl oz water and a little flour and mix to a dough. If using dry yeast, blend the yeast with the 400ml/14 fl oz water, add a little flour and pour into the well. Sprinkle a little flour on top and leave to rise in a warm place for 12 hours. • Mix the milk with the rest of the water and the salt and combine with this starter and the rest of the flours to form a workable dough. Cover and leave to rise for 1 hour. • Knead the dough thoroughly again, place in the oiled tin and leave to rise for a further hour. • Make a 5mm/¼in deep cut lengthways in the dough and brush the top with the melted butter. Preheat the oven to 230°C/450°F/Gas Mark 8. Place a cupful of water in the base of the oven. Bake the bread on the bottom shelf for 50 minutes.

Coarse Mixed Grain Bread

All of these grains are obtainable at health food shops. Try combining different grains, while keeping the same proportions of wheat flour

Quantities for 2 loaves:

250g/8oz cracked wheat
150g/5¹/₂oz porridge oats
2 tbsps sourdough
1 sachet dry yeast
750ml/1¹/₄ pints water
100g/4oz rye flakes
350g/11oz wholemeal rye flour
350g/11oz wholewheat flour
1 tsp salt
Butter for the baking sheet

Preparation time: 40 minutes
Rising time: 13 hours or overnight
Baking time: 1³/₄ to 2 hours
Nutritional Value:
Analysis per slice, if divided into 60 slices, approx:
• 185kJ/45kcal
• 2g protein
• 0g fat
• 9g carbohydrate

To make the starter, combine the cracked wheat and oats with the sourdough, the dry yeast and 250ml/9 fl oz lukewarm water. Leave in a warm place for 12 hours. • Soak the rye flakes in 8 tbsps hot water for 12 hours or overnight. • Combine the rye and wholewheat flours with the salt, the soaked rye and the remaining water and knead this into the starter. If the dough is too soft, add more wholewheat flour. Cover the dough and leave to rise for at least 45 minutes. • Butter a baking sheet. • Flour your hands and shape the dough into two long loaves and place them on the baking sheet. Brush the loaves with a little water and bake on the bottom shelf of a preheated 225°C/450°C/Gas Mark 8 oven for 30 minutes. Then reduce the temperature to 180°C/350°F/Gas Mark 4 and bake for a further 1¹/₄ to 1¹/₂ hours. • Cool on a wire rack.

Rye Bread in a Roasting Bag

Baking in a roasting bag gives this bread a very special aroma

Quantities for 1 loaf:

500g/1lb 2oz wholewheat flour

1.2kg/2 lb 11 oz rye flour

120g/4oz sourdough or starter (see page 8)

7g/¹/₄oz dry yeast

1l/1³/₄ pints lukewarm water

1 tbsp salt

1 tsp golden syrup or honey

¹/₂ tsp each crushed aniseed, fennel and coriander seed

6 tbsps sunflower seeds

FOR THE DECORATION:

1 tbsp rye flakes

¹/₂ tbsp crushed dill

Preparation time: 40 minutes
Rising time: 13-14 hours
Baking time: 1¹/₂ hours
Nutritional value:
Analysis per slice, if divided into 30 slices, approx:
- 710kJ/170kcal
- 5g protein
- 2g fat
- 36g carbohydrate

To make the starter, combine half the rye flour, the sourdough or starter, the dry yeast and the lukewarm water. • Put the rest of the rye flour in a large bowl, make a well in the centre and pour in the yeast mixture. • Cover and leave to rise in a warm place for at least 12 hours. • Add the salt, golden syrup or honey, spices and sunflower seeds to the yeast mixture. Work in the remaining flour and knead to a workable dough. If necessary, add a little more lukewarm water. • Shape the dough into a ball, return it to the bowl, cover with a damp cloth and leave to rise in a warm place for about 1¹/₂ hours. The dough should ferment and air bubbles should form. • Knead the dough thoroughly once again, wet your hands and shape it into three long loaves. Brush with a little water. Combine the coarsely-ground rye and spices and sprinkle these over the dough. • Slide the dough into roasting bags. Seal the bags tightly but use a needle to pierce holes in the top of the bag to allow steam to escape. • Place the breads on a cold baking sheet and bake on a low shelf in a preheated 230°C/450°F/Gas Mark 8 oven for 1¹/₂ hours. • Remove the breads from the bags and cool on wire racks. Wait at least 12 hours before slicing, to allow the flavour of the spices to develop.

Our Tip: Even when thoroughly kneaded, a dough made of wholemeal flours should always be somewhat sticky. Since the amount of liquid needed for making bread varies with the quality of the flours, you may need to add more liquid or flour. Experience will tell you when you have exactly the right consistency.

Bread made from high-gluten American flours will always need additional liquid.
This bread can also be baked in oiled, square baking tins or loaf tins. If using loaf tins, make a long gash down the centre of each loaf and sprinkle with sesame seeds before baking.

Tasty Bread in a Basket

Oval and round reed and cane baskets are available in a variety of sizes which are suitable for bread baking

Quantities for 2 baskets, each approx. 15cm/6in in diameter:

400g/14oz wholemeal rye flour
350g/11oz wholewheat flour
1 tsp coriander
$^1/_2$ tsp fennel
$^1/_2$ tsp caraway seeds
42g/1$^1/_2$oz fresh yeast or 21g/$^3/_4$oz dry yeast
2 tbsps sugar
250ml/9 fl oz lukewarm water
80g/3oz sourdough
3 tsps salt
Flour for the baskets
Oil for greasing the baking sheet

Preparation time: 40 minutes
Rising time: 2$^3/_4$ hours
Baking time: 1 hour
Nutritional Value:
Analysis per slice, if divided into 40 slices, approx:
• 500kJ/120kcal
• 4g protein
• 1g fat
• 26g carbohydrate

Mix the flours in a bowl. Crush the coriander, fennel and caraway seeds with a pestle and mortar. • Mix the crumbled fresh yeast or the dry yeast with the sugar and 125ml/4 fl oz water and set aside to froth. • Combine the starter dough, sourdough, salt and crushed spices and add to the flour. • Knead the dough thoroughly, cover and leave to rise in a warm place for at least 30 minutes. • Dust the baskets with flour. • Knead the dough thoroughly again and divide into 2 portions. Fill each basket with 1 portion of dough, cover the baskets with a cloth and leave to rise for 1$^1/_2$ hours. • Brush the baking sheet with oil. Place an ovenproof dish of cold water in the base of the oven. • Turn out the loaves onto the baking sheet and bake on a low shelf in a preheated 230°C/450°F/Gas Mark 8 for 10 minutes. Remove the dish from the oven, reduce the temperature to 220°C/425°F/Gas Mark 7 and continue to bake the bread for 45 minutes. • Switch off and leave the bread in the oven for 5 minutes. Cool on a wire rack.

Norwegian Country Bread

A tangy, dark bread for lovers of wholefood

Quantities for 2 x 900g/2lb loaf tins:

FOR THE STARTER DOUGH:

500g/1lb 2oz rye flour

42g/1½oz fresh yeast or 21g/¾oz dry yeast

500ml/18 fl oz lukewarm buttermilk

1 tbsp golden syrup

FOR THE BREAD DOUGH:

200g/7oz wholewheat flour

75g/3oz golden syrup

2 tsps sea salt

1 tbsp ground cardamom seed

Butter for the tins

Preparation time: 50 minutes
Rising time: 4 hours
Baking time: 1 hour 5 minutes
Nutritional value:
Analysis per slice, if divided into 30 slices, approx:
- 335kJ/80kcal
- 3g protein
- 1g fat
- 17g carbohydrate

To make the starter dough, pour the rye flour into a bowl and make a well in the centre. Add the yeast to the buttermilk, stir with the golden syrup and pour into the well and mix with a little of the flour. • Sprinkle some more flour on top. Cover and leave to rise in a warm place for 1hour or until foaming and slightly risen. • To make the bread dough, add the wholewheat flour to the starter dough. Add the golden and stir well. Add the salt and cardamom seeds and knead to a workable, slightly moist dough, adding more water if necessary. Leave to rise for 3 hours or until doubled in bulk. • Butter the baking sheet. Divide the dough into two pieces and put it in the buttered tins. Smooth over the tops. Cover with a damp cloth and leave to prove until the dough has increased in bulk by about one-third. This will take about an hour. • Bake the bread on the bottom shelf of a preheated 200°C/400°F/Gas Mark 6 oven for about 50 minutes. It should be golden-brown and come away from the tin on all sides. If the bread browns too quickly, cover it with greased baking paper after 40 minutes. • Turn the oven off and leave the bread to rest for 15 minutes. • Remove the bread from the tins, spray it or brush it all over with cold water and leave to cool on a wire rack. The flavour of the bread will take 24 hours to develop fully, by which time the bread will be easy to slice.

Our Tip: Stored in a cool and well-ventilated place, this bread will stay fresh for up to a week. It is most delicious spread simply with butter, but cheese, cream cheese with herbs, Cheddar cheese with radishes or chopped gherkins, ham, salami or smoked salmon also make good toppings. If you prefer bread that is less sweet, replace the 75g/3oz golden syrup with 75g/3oz bitter chocolate. You can sprinkle the loaves with caraway seeds or brush them with an egg yolk mixed with 3 tbsps water before baking.

Crusty Sesame Bread

Although rising time is long, it means that the bread can be left overnight and baked in the morning, ready for breakfast.

Finnish Spiced Bread

Aromatic spices and beer give this bread its characteristic flavour

Quantities for 2 loaves:

500g/1lb 2oz rye flakes
2 tbsps sourdough mix
750ml/1¼ pints lukewarm water
250g/8oz wheatmeal flour
500g/1lb 2oz rye flour
2 packets dry yeast
4 tbsps sesame seeds
1 tbsp salt
Baking paper for the baking sheet

Preparation time: 45 minutes
Rising time: 13 hours
Baking time: 40 minutes
Nutritional value:
Analysis per slice, if divided into 50 slices, approx
- 335kJ/80kcal
- 2g protein
- 1g fat
- 16g carbohydrate

Combine the rye flakes, the sourdough mix and 500ml/18 fl oz water. Cover and leave for 12 hours at room temperature. Add the rest of the lukewarm water, both types of flour, the dry yeast, 3 tbsps sesame seeds and the salt to the starter dough. Knead to a workable dough. If the dough is too wet, add more wheatmeal flour. • Cover and leave to rise in a warm place for 1 hour. • Line the baking sheet with greaseproof paper. • Flour your hands and shape the dough into 2 long loaves, place them on the baking sheet, brush with cold water and sprinkle with the remaining sesame seeds. • Bake the bread on the bottom shelf of a preheated 200°C/400°F/Gas Mark 6 oven for 40 minutes. Cool on a wire rack.

Quantities for 12.5cm/10in loaf:

750g/1lb 11oz rye flour
63g/2 ½oz fresh yeast or 32g/1oz dry yeast
½ tsp sugar
125ml/4 fl oz light ale or lager
75g/3oz butter
75g/3oz syrup or honey
250g/8oz wholewheat flour
250ml/9 fl oz lukewarm water
2 tsps salt
½ tsp each ground ginger, cloves, cinnamon and nutmeg
2 tsps grated orange peel
Butter for the loaf tin

Preparation time: 40 minutes
Rising time: 3 hours
Baking time: 50 minutes
Nutritional value:
Analysis per slice, if divided into 20 slices, approx:
- 840kJ/200kcal
- 4g protein
- 4g fat
- 36g carbohydrate

Crumble the fresh yeast into the centre of the rye flour and sprinkle on the sugar. Warm the beer and mix all but 3 tbsps with the yeast and a little flour. If using dry yeast, mix the yeast with the beer and sugar and then pour it into the centre of the flour. Cover and leave to rise until the dough has doubled in bulk, about 2 hours. • Warm the butter with the syrup or honey until melted and leave to cool. • Mix the starter dough with all the flour; add the butter and syrup mixture, water and salt and knead well. Cover and leave to rise for 1 hour. Then knead the dough, put it in the buttered tin, cover and leave to rise until doubled in bulk. • Brush the bread with the remaining beer and bake on the centre shelf of a preheated 220°C/425°F/Gas Mark 7 oven for 50 minutes.

Walnut Bread

This is an unusual and delicious bread

Quantities for 1 wide, 35cm/14in loaf tin:

500g/1lb 2oz wholewheat flour
400g/12oz wheatmeal flour
250g/8oz strong plain white flour
60g/2oz sourdough mix
1 tsp dry yeast
750ml/1 ¼ pints lukewarm water
2 tsps salt
½ tsp sugar
250g/8oz shelled walnuts
Butter or oil for the tin

Preparation time: 1 hour
Rising time: 13-14 hours
Baking time: 1 hour
Nutritional value:
Analysis per slice, if divided into 30 slices, approx:
• 750kJ/180kcal
• 5g protein
• 6g fat
• 25g carbohydrate

Combine the wholewheat flour, 250g/8oz of the wheatmeal and the white flours in a bowl and make a well in the centre. Place the sourdough, yeast and half the water in the well and combine with a little of the flour. • Dissolve the salt and sugar in the remaining water, mix with the starter dough and flour and knead to a workable dough. Cover and leave to rise in a warm place for 12 hours. Finely grind 50g/2oz of the walnuts and coarsely chop the remainder. • Butter or oil the tin. • Knead the dough thoroughly again and incorporate the rest of the wheatmeal flour and the ground and chopped nuts. • Shape the dough into a loaf, place it in the tin, cover and leave to rise until increased in bulk by one-third. This will take 1 to 2 hours. • Bake the bread on a low shelf of a preheated 220°C/425°F/Gas Mark 7 oven for 1 hour. • Check, by rapping the bottom of the loaf, to see if the bread is baked through and leave to cool on a wire rack.

Rye Potato Bread

This bread is very dark despite the potato content

Quantities for 1 30cm/12in baking tin:

FOR THE STARTER DOUGH:
200g/7oz rye flour	
2 tsps dry yeast	
400ml/14 fl oz lukewarm water	
2 tsps clear honey	

FOR THE BREAD DOUGH:
500g/1lb 2oz floury potatoes	
350g/11oz wholewheat flour	
50g/2oz soya flour	
200ml/7 fl oz lukewarm water	
1 tsp each caraway seeds, sea salt and dried marjoram	
Butter for the tin	

Preparation time: 40 minutes
Rising time: 26 hours
Baking time: 1 hour 5 minutes
Nutritional value:
Analysis per slice, if divided into 30 slices, approx:
- 290kJ/70kcal
- 3g protein
- 1g fat
- 14g carbohydrate

To make the starter dough, mix the rye flour with the dry yeast, water and honey. • Cover with a cloth and leave for at least 24 hours in a warm place at 24°C/75°F. By this time the dough should clearly be fermenting and will resemble a pale, fluffy foam. • Prior to baking the bread, scrub the potatoes under running water and boil them in their skins for 30-35 minutes or until soft. • Peel the cooked potatoes immediately and grate them. • Mix the grated potato into the starter dough. • Add the wholewheat flour to the starter dough, together with the caraway seeds, salt and crushed marjoram. Knead to a workable dough. • Butter the tin, place the dough in it and smooth the top with a spatula. Leave the dough to rise in a warm place until it has increased in bulk by one-third. This will take 1 to 2 hours. • Place the tin on the bottom shelf of a preheated 200°C/400°F/Gas Mark

6 oven and bake for 50 minutes or until golden-brown. Then turn off the oven and leave the bread to rest in the oven for a further 15 minutes. • Remove the rye potato bread from the tin, spray the top with cold water and leave to cool on a wire rack.

Our Tip: Leave the bread for 24 hours before slicing. When a little stale it is delicious toasted. If you enjoy experimenting, try making this bread with grated courgette, beetroot or carrot. Use the same quantity as for potato, i.e. 500g/1lb 2oz. It may be necessary to adjust the amount of added liquid.

Plain White Bread

This golden-brown crusty bread can be made as a batch or a loaf

Quantities for 1 batch or 1 24cm/10in loaf tin:

42g/1½oz fresh yeast or 21g/¾oz dry yeast
1 tbsp sugar
500ml-750ml/1-1¼ pints lukewarm water
1.3kg/2lb 15oz strong plain flour
3-4 tsps salt
FOR THE GLAZE:
2 tbsps milk
2 tbsps stout or malt beer
Butter for tin and baking sheet

Preparation time: 40 minutes
Rising time: 3 hours
Baking time: 50 minutes for the tin, 35-40 minutes for the batch
Nutritional value:
Analysis per slice, if divided into 40 slices, approx:
• 460kJ/110kcal
• 4g protein
• 0g fat
• 24g carbohydrate

Crumble the fresh yeast and blend the fresh or dry yeast with the sugar and 100ml/4 fl oz lukewarm water. Cover and leave to froth in a warm place for 15 minutes. • Sift the flour into a large bowl. Add the dissolved yeast, salt and remaining water. Knead the dough well until it leaves the bowl clean and is smooth and elastic. Cover and leave to rise in a warm place for 2 hours or until doubled in bulk. • Butter the baking sheet and loaf tin. • Knead the dough again and divide in two. Half fill the tin with dough and smooth the surface using a wet metal spatula or palette knife. Shape the remaining dough into a long batch, about 6cm/2in in diameter, and place on the baking sheet. Cover and leave both loaves to prove for a further 45 minutes. The dough in the tin should almost have reached the top of the tin by this time. • Place an ovenproof dish of cold water in the base of the oven. • Using a

sharp knife, make a long, ½cm/¼in deep cut lengthways in the dough in the loaf tin and brush the top with milk. Make 4 or 5 cuts across the top of the batch and brush with the malt beer or stout. • Bake the bread on the centre shelf of a preheated 220°C/425°F/Gas Mark 7 oven for 45 minutes. After 10 minutes remove the water from the oven and reduce the temperature to 200°C/400°F/Gas Mark 6. • Take the batch out of the oven after 35-40 minutes and leave to cool on a wire rack. • Bake the loaf tin for a further 10 minutes and leave to rest in the oven for 5 minutes after the oven has been switched off. • Remove from the tin and leave to cool on a wire rack. • This white bread tastes best when eaten straight from the oven. White bread that has been stored in a cool place can be reheated briefly in the oven or made into toast.

Savoury Loaves

A tasty party snack which, like the white bread, is best served fresh from the oven

Quantities for 3 long loaves:

300g/10oz wholewheat flour
200g/8oz wheatmeal flour
50g/2oz cornmeal or semolina
1 tsp freshly ground coriander
1 tsp sweet paprika powder
2 tsps salt
42g/1½oz fresh yeast or 21g/¾oz dry yeast
1 tbsp clear honey
175ml/6 fl oz lukewarm water
100g/4oz streaky bacon, rinds removed
2 onions
2 garlic cloves
2 tbsps sunflower seed oil
250g/8oz low-fat curd cheese

FOR THE WORK SURFACE:

2-3 tbsps cornmeal or semolina
Butter for the baking sheet

Preparation time: 1 hour
Rising time: 1 hour
Baking time: 30 minutes

Nutritional value:

Analysis per loaf, approx:
- 4110kJ/980kcal
- 39g protein
- 32g fat
- 140g carbohydrate

Put the flours into a large bowl with the cornmeal or semolina, coriander, paprika and salt. Make a well in the centre, crumble the fresh yeast into the well, mix with the honey and wait for 2 minutes until the yeast has dissolved. • Mix the water and a little flour with the fresh yeast and sprinkle a little flour on top. If using dry yeast, blend the yeast with the honey, water and a little flour and sprinkle some flour on top. Cover and leave in a warm place at about 22°C/70°F until cracks appear in the flour. • Dice the bacon, chop the onions and crush the garlic. • Heat the oil in a frying pan, fry the bacon until crispy and remove from the pan.

• Fry the onion and garlic in the bacon fat until golden-brown and remove from the heat. • Add the curd cheese to the starter dough together with all the flour and knead well. Cover and leave for 20 minutes. • Knead the dough thoroughly again and incorporate the bacon, onion and garlic. If the dough is too firm, add a little water; if it is too soft to leave the bowl clean, add a little more wholewheat flour. • Butter the baking sheet. • Divide the dough into 3 large slices and shape each slice into a long, thin loaf, about 30cm/12in in length. • Sprinkle the cornmeal on the work surface, roll each loaf in it, place on the baking sheet and flatten down a little. Cover and leave to rise until increased in bulk by one-third. • Bake the bread on the centre shelf of a preheated 200°C/400°F/Gas Mark 6 oven for 30 minutes until golden-brown. • Remove from the oven, spray with a cold water and leave to cool on a wire rack.

Herbed Oaten Bread

Buttermilk can be used instead of full cream milk

Quantities for 1 loaf:
400g/14oz wheatmeal flour
120g/4oz oats
1 packet dry yeast
1 tsp sugar
2 tsps celery salt
1 bunch each of fresh dill weed, parsley and chives
750ml/1¹/₄ pints lukewarm full cream milk
1 tbsp condensed milk
Butter for the baking sheet

Preparation time: 30 minutes
Rising time: about 1 hour
Baking time: 30-40 minutes
Nutritional value:
Analysis per slice, if divided into 30 slices, approx:
• 290kJ/70kcal
• 2g protein
• 1g fat
• 13g carbohydrate

Mix the flour, oats, yeast, sugar and celery salt together. •
Finely chop the herbs and add to the flour mixture together with the milk. Knead until the dough leaves the bowl clean. • Cover and leave to rise until the dough has almost doubled in bulk – this will take about 40 minutes. • Turn the dough out onto a lightly floured surface and knead well. Shape the dough into a long loaf and smooth the top with your hands. Butter the baking sheet, place the dough on it and cover and leave to rise for 20 minutes. • Make 4 ¹/₂cm/¹/₄in cuts across the top of the loaf, brush with the condensed milk and bake on the centre shelf of a preheated 200°C/400°F/Gas Mark 6 oven for 30-40 minutes until golden-brown.

Wheaten Toast Bread

This bread is also delicious eaten fresh

Quantities for 2 25cm/10in baking tins:
21g/³/₄oz fresh yeast or 10g/¹/₄oz dry yeast
1 tbsp sugar
500ml/18 fl oz lukewarm milk
800g/1lb 12oz wheatmeal flour
2 tsps salt
50g/2oz soft butter
Butter for the tins

Preparation time: 40 minutes
Rising time: 2 hours
Baking time: 40 minutes
Nutritional value:
Analysis per slice, if divided into 40 slices, approx:
• 375kJ/90kcal
• 3g protein
• 2g fat
• 15g carbohydrate

Crumble the fresh yeast and mix the fresh or dry yeast with the sugar and 100ml/4 fl oz milk. Cover and leave to froth in a warm place for 15 minutes. • Sift the flour into a bowl. Add the yeast mixture, the remaining milk, salt and butter and knead to a workable dough. Cover and leave to rise in a warm place for 1 hour. • Butter the baking tins. • Knead the dough again, divide into 2 portions, place in the tins, smooth the top, cover and leave to rise for a further 45 minutes. • Make one long ¹/₂cm/¹/₄in cut along the length of the loaf and bake on the bottom shelf of a preheated 200°C/400°F/Gas Mark 6 oven for 30 minutes. • Remove the bread from the tins and leave for 10 minutes in the oven after it has been switched off. • Leave to cool on a wire rack.

Three-Grain Luxury Toast Bread

All these flours can be found in healthfood shops

Quantities for 1 25cm/10in baking tin:
200g/7oz barley flour
100g/4oz wholemeal flour
100g/4oz buckwheat flour
42g/1½oz fresh yeast or 21g/¾oz dry yeast
½ tbsp clear honey
200ml/7 fl oz cream
5 tbsps hot water
1 tsp sea salt
Butter for the baking tin

Preparation time: 35 minutes
Rising time: 1¼ hours
Baking time: 40 minutes
Nutritional value:
Analysis per slice, if divided into 25 slices, approx:
• 335kJ/80kcal
• 2g protein
• 3g fat
• 11g carbohydrate

Combine the flours in a large bowl. • Make a well in the centre, crumble in the fresh yeast, pour on the honey and wait for 2 minutes until the yeast has dissolved. Mix the cream with the hot water, pour onto the yeast and incorporate a little flour. If using dry yeast, blend the yeast with the honey, cream and hot water and then pour this mixture into the well and mix in a little flour. Add the salt to the yeast mixture and knead until the dough leaves the sides of the bowl clean. • Cover and leave to rise for 90 minutes. • Butter the baking tin. • Knead the dough thoroughly again and, if necessary, add a little extra flour. Put the dough in the tin, smooth the top, cover with a damp cloth and leave to prove for 30 minutes or until increased in bulk by one-third. • Bake the bread on the centre shelf of a preheated 200°C/400°F/Gas Mark 6 oven for 30 minutes or until golden-brown. • Leave the bread to cool in the tin for 10 minutes and then take it out, spray it all over with a little cold water and leave on a wire rack to cool. • Wait a day before slicing the bread.

Wholemeal Soya Bread

This bread stays fresh for 3 days and is then delicious as toast

Quantities for 1 loaf:

400g/14oz wholewheat flour
200g/7oz rye flour
200g/7oz soya flour
42g/1½oz fresh yeast or
21g/¾oz dry yeast
1 tbsp clear honey
500ml/18 fl oz lukewarm water
2 tsps sea salt

FOR THE WORK SURFACE:

50g/2oz raw sesame seeds
Butter for the baking sheet

Preparation time: 25 minutes
Rising time: 1 hour
Baking time: 40 minutes
Nutritional value:
Analysis per slice, if divided into
20 slices, approx:
- 630kJ/150kcal
- 7g protein
- 4g fat
- 21g carbohydrate

Finely grind the wheat and rye grains and mix with the soya in a bowl. • Make a well in the centre, crumble in the fresh yeast, pour on the honey and wait 2 minutes for the yeast to dissolve. • Mix the water and a little flour with the starter dough. Cover and leave to rise for 15 minutes. If using dry yeast, blend the yeast with the honey, water and a little flour, pour this mixture into the well in the flour and then cover and leave to rise for 15 minutes. Then knead again and if necessary add a little more water or wheatmeal flour. • Butter the baking sheet. • Sprinkle the sesame seeds on the work surface and roll the dough into a ball, pressing the seeds in gently. • Place the ball of dough on the baking sheet, press to flatten, cover and leave to rise until it has increased in bulk by about one-third. • Bake the bread in a preheated 220°C/425°F/Gas Mark 7 oven for 30 minutes or until golden-brown and leave to stand in the oven for a further 10 minutes after the oven has been switched off. • Spray the bread with cold water and leave to cool on a wire rack.

Six-Grain Bread

Try as many different types of flour as you can find, but keep the same quantity of wheat flour

Quantities for 1 loaf:

250g/8oz wholemeal rye flour

750g/1lb 11oz wholewheat flour

FOR THE STARTER:

2 packages dry yeast

1 tsp brown sugar

50g/2 oz wholewheat flour

50g/2oz rolled oats

50g/2oz barley flour

50g/2oz millet flakes

50g/2oz buckwheat flour

$^{1}/_{2}$ tsp salt

2 tbsps pinhead oatmeal

Baking or greaseproof paper for the baking sheet

Preparation time: 1 hour
Rising time: 2¾ hours
Baking time: 1 hour 20 min
Nutritional value:
Analysis per slice, if divided into 30 slices, approx:
• 585kJ/140kcal
• 5g protein
• 1g fat
• 28g carbohydrate

Combine the rye and wheatmeal flour in a large bowl and make a well in the centre. To make the starter, mix 250ml/9 fl oz lukewarm water with yeast in a small bowl. Add the sugar and the wholewheat flour. Cover with a damp cloth and leave in a warm place for 20 minutes, or until well risen. Add the rest of the flours, except the pinhead oatmeal, and sprinkle with the salt. Add another 250ml/9 fl oz lukewarm water and leave to rise again for 20 minutes. Then add the starter to the well in the flours in the bowl. Add enough lukewarm water (about 250ml/9 fl oz) to make a fairly firm dough. Knead well until the dough leaves the sides of the bowl clean • Shape the dough into a round batch and place on a baking sheet lined with greaseproof paper. Remove the base from a springform tin. Butter the ring and place it round the dough. Cover and leave to rise in a warm place for 2 hours. • Remove the ring. Sprinkle a baking sheet with 1 tbsp of the oatmeal. Lay the loaf on top of it. Cut a grid pattern into the top of the dough. Brush the dough with a little water and sprinkle with the rest of the pinhead oatmeal. • Cover with a sheet of baking or greaseproof paper and place on the bottom shelf of a preheated 220°C/425°F/Gas Mark 7 oven. Bake the bread for 40 minutes or until it sounds hollow when rapped on the bottom. • Remove the baking or greaseproof paper and bake the bread for a further 40 minutes. • Place on a wire rack to cool. Leave for at least 8 hours before slicing.

Our Tip: You can also add cracked wheat, soaked for four hours, to the dough mixture. You will then need to add less water. Instead of pinhead oatmeal, sprinkle with semolina or cornmeal.

Light Poppyseed Bread

This dough can also be made into crusty rolls

Quantities for 1 35cm/14in baking tin:

100g/4oz black poppy seeds	
750g/1lb 11oz wheat grains	
2 tsps ground caraway seeds	
50g/2oz very fine soya flour	
2 tsps sea salt	
42g/1½oz fresh yeast or 21g/¾oz dry yeast	
1 tsp clear honey	
250ml/9 fl oz lukewarm milk	
250ml/9 fl oz lukewarm water	
Butter for the tin	

Preparation time: 40 minutes
Rising time: about 1 hour
Baking time: 45 minutes
Nutritional value:
Analysis per slice, if divided into 30 slices, approx:
• 420kJ/100kcal
• 4g protein
• 3g fat
• 16g carbohydrate

Roast the poppy seeds over a medium heat in a dry, heavy frying pan, stirring all the time until they start to crackle and give off an aroma. • Finely grind the wheat grains and set 50g/2oz of them aside. • Put the rest in a bowl and mix with the caraway seeds, soya flour, salt and toasted poppy seeds. Make a well in the centre, crumble in the fresh yeast, pour on the honey and wait 2 minutes for the yeast to dissolve. • Pour the lukewarm milk and water onto the yeast and mix to a starter dough. If using dry yeast, blend the yeast with the honey, lukewarm milk and water and then pour into the well in the flour and mix to a starter dough. Cover and leave to rise in a warm place at about 22°C/70°F for 15 minutes. • Mix the remaining flour in the bowl into the starter dough and knead well. Cover and leave the dough to rise again in a warm place for 20 minutes. • Knead the dough thoroughly once again. If it

is too firm, add a little more milk; if it is too soft and does not leave the bowl clean, incorporate a little more wholewheat flour. • Grease the baking tin with butter. • Turn the dough out on a work surface, sprinkle with the remaining wheatmeal flour and shape the dough into a 35cm/14in loaf. Place the dough in the tin, flatten gently, cover and leave to rise until increased in bulk by about one-third. This will take about 25-30 minutes. • Bake on the bottom shelf of a preheated 200°C/400°F/Gas Mark 6 oven for 45 minutes until golden-brown. Leave to rest in the oven for 10 minutes after the oven has been switched off. • Remove the bread from the tin, spray all over with cold water and leave on a wire rack to cool.

Our Tip: This bread will keep fresh for about 3 days. It is delicious spread with butter and jam or honey. Mild cheeses such as Cheddar, Gouda or cream cheese are also a good accompaniment.

Special Breads

If you like experimenting with new recipes, you will enjoy trying some of these special breads

Courgette and Apple Bread

illustrated left

Quantities for 1 30cm/12in loaf:

300g/10oz courgettes
1 medium-sized apple
300g/10oz wheatmeal flour
3 tsps baking powder
5 eggs
100ml/4 fl oz olive oil
1 tsp salt
150g/5½oz freshly grated Cheddar cheese
50g/2oz pumpkin seeds
Butter for the tin

Preparation time: 20 minutes
Baking time: 1 hour 10 min
Nutritional value:
Analysis per slice, if divided into 30 slices, approx:
- 540kJ/130kcal
- 6g protein
- 9g fat
- 8g carbohydrate

Butter the loaf tin. • Coarsely grate the courgette and apple. • Combine the flour, baking powder, eggs, oil, salt, cheese and grated courgette and apple to form a wet dough. Add the pumpkin seeds. • Put the dough in the loaf tin and bake in a preheated 200°C/400°F/Gas Mark 6 oven for 50 minutes. • Reduce the heat to 180°C/350°F/Gas Mark 4 and continue to bake for a further 20 minutes. Leave the bread to cool in the tin, then loosen the edges all the way around using a knife and turn the bread out onto a wire rack.

Our Tip: This apple and courgette bread is very tempting served with raw ham, tomato salad, tzatziki (or cucumber raitha) and wine.

Portuguese Corn Bread

illustrated right

Quantities for 1 30cm/12in tin:

42g/1½oz fresh yeast or 21g/¾oz dry yeast
Pinch of sugar
200ml/7 fl oz lukewarm water
250g/8oz cornmeal
1 tsp salt
200ml/7 fl oz boiling water
1 tbsp olive oil
250g/8oz wheatmeal flour
Butter for the tin

Preparation time: 30 minutes
Rising time: 1¼ hours
Baking time: 40 minutes
Nutritional value:
Analysis per slice, if divided into 25 slices, approx:
- 315kJ/75kcal
- 2g protein
- 1g fat
- 15g carbohydrate

Crumble the fresh yeast, sprinkle the fresh or dry yeast with the sugar and mix with the water. Cover and leave to froth until the cornmeal mixture (see below) has cooled. • Mix 200g/7oz of the cornmeal with the salt and boiling water and leave to cool for 10 minutes. • Add the yeast mixture, the remaining cornmeal, the oil and the wheatmeal flour to the cornmeal mixture and mix well. Knead the dough until soft and elastic, cover and leave to rise for 30 minutes, then knead well and, if necessary, add a little more wheatmeal flour. • Put the dough in the greased baking tin, cover and leave to rise for a further 30 minutes. • Brush the bread with water and bake in a preheated 200°C/400°F/Gas Mark 6 oven for 40 minutes until golden-brown.

Wholemeal Curd Cheese Bread

A delicious breakfast-time bread.

Quantities for 1 loaf:

600g/1lb 5oz wheat grains	
42g/1½oz fresh yeast or 21g/¾oz dry yeast	
1 tbsp clear honey	
100ml/4 fl oz lukewarm water	
2 tsps sea salt	
500g/1lb 2oz low fat curd or cottage cheese	
2 tbsps sunflower oil	
Butter for the baking sheet	

Preparation time: 30 minutes
Rising time: 1 hour
Baking time: 50 minutes
Nutritional value:
Analysis per slice, if divided into 30 slices, approx:
- 335kJ/80kcal
- 5g protein
- 1g fat
- 13g carbohydrate

Grind half the wheat grains to fine flour; grind the other half coarsely. Combine in a large bowl. • Make a well in the centre and crumble in the fresh yeast; pour on the honey and wait 2 minutes for the yeast to dissolve. • Add the lukewarm water to the yeast and mix, incorporating a little flour to form a wet starter dough. If using dry yeast, blend the yeast with the honey and water before pouring into the well. Sprinkle a little flour on the starter dough, cover and leave to rise in a warm place at about 22°C/70°F until cracks can clearly be seen. This will take about 20 minutes. Add the salt, curd cheese and oil to the starter dough and knead all ingredients with all the flour to a workable dough. Cover and leave to rise again in a warm place for 20 minutes. • Butter the baking sheet. • Knead the dough thoroughly again. If it is too firm, add a little more water; if it is too soft, add a little more wholewheat flour. • Shape the dough into a ball, place on the baking sheet and flatten until it is 20cm/8in thick. • Cover and leave to rise for a further 20 minutes until the loaf has increased in bulk by about one-third. • Bake the bread on the centre shelf of a preheated 200°C/400°F/Gas Mark 6 oven for about 40 minutes until golden-brown and leave to rest for 10 minutes with the oven switched off. • Place the bread on a wire rack, spray all over with a little cold water and leave to cool. • One hour later, the bread will be ready to serve. It is best served fresh with butter and honey or jam or mild cheese.

Our Tip: The crust of wholemeal bread is never as smooth as that of bread made with refined flour and should always be sprayed or brushed with cold water before being allowed to cool. Bakers used to use fat, compact brushes for this purpose. A plant spray with a fine nozzle is an excellent substitute. The water can also be brushed on. Spraying or brushing bread with cold water makes it easier to slice once cool and gives it an appealing, golden-brown glaze.

Vegetable Panettone

A savoury variation on the famous Italian Christmas cake-bread

Quantities for 1 panettone tin or 1 tall 1.5l/2¹/₂ pint tin:

21g/³/₄oz fresh yeast or 10g/¹/₄oz dry yeast
1 tsp sugar
Pinch of saffron
250ml/9 fl oz warm milk
1 tbsp butter
1 tsp salt
1 egg
400g/14oz wheatmeal flour
50g/2oz skinned, ground almonds
100g/4oz each of carrots and broccoli spears
¹/₂ red pepper
Butter for the tin

Preparation time: 40 minutes
Rising time: 1¹/₂ hours
Baking time: 45 minutes
Nutritional value:
Analysis per slice, if divided into 16 slices, approx:
- 454kJ/130kcal
- 5g protein
- 4g fat
- 21g carbohydrate

Crumble the fresh yeast and mix the fresh or dry yeast with the sugar and 3 tbsps lukewarm water. Cover and leave to rise in a warm place for 15 minutes. • Soak the saffron in the milk, melt the butter in the mixture and stir in the salt, egg, flour, ground almonds and the yeast mixture. Knead to a workable dough. Cover and leave to rise for 40 minutes. • Wash and trim the vegetables, blanch for 3 minutes, drain and cool. Chop finely and add to the dough. Butter the tin, fill it with the dough, make some diagonal cuts in the top of the dough and leave to rise for another 30 minutes. • Bake the panettone on a low shelf in a preheated 220°C/425°F/Gas Mark 5 oven for 45 minutes. After 5 minutes reduce the temperature to 180°C/350°F/Gas Mark 4. • Remove from the tin, leave to cool on a wire rack and serve with butter.

Tasty Sauerkraut Bread

Try adding some chopped fried bacon or pork crackling and caraway seeds to the sauerkraut for a very special filling

Quantities for 1 25cm/10in baking tin:

21g/³/₄oz fresh yeast or 10g/¹/₄oz dry yeast
1 tbsp golden syrup
200g/7oz wheatmeal flour
200g/7oz rye flour
1¹/₂ tsp salt
200ml/7 fl oz malt beer or stout
2 medium onions
250g/4oz sauerkraut
2 tbsps pork dripping or lard
Pinch of black pepper
Pork dripping or lard for the tin

Preparation time: 30 minutes
Rising time: 1¹/₄ hours
Baking time: 1 hour
Nutritional value:
Analysis per slice, if divided into 20 slices, approx:
- 355kJ/85kcal
- 2g protein
- 1g fat
- 15g carbohydrate

Mix the fresh or dry yeast with the sugar beet syrup and 2 tbsps lukewarm water and leave to froth for 5 minutes. Then add the flour, 1 tsp salt and the beer or stout and knead thoroughly. If necessary, add up to 2 tsps more water. • Sprinkle a little flour on top of the dough, cover and leave to rise for 1 hour, until it has doubled in bulk. • Cut the onions into strips. Chop the sauerkraut. • Fry the onions in the dripping or lard until golden-brown. Add the sauerkraut and fry for about 8 minutes, stirring frequently, until the liquid has been absorbed. Season with the remaining salt and pepper. • Knead the dough well again, divide into 3 portions and roll out to the size of the tin. Put the dough and the lukewarm sauerkraut mixture into the tin in alternating layers. • Cover and leave to rise for 30 minutes. • Bake the bread for about 1 hour on the bottom shelf of a preheated 190°C/375°F/Gas Mark 5 oven.

Our Tip: You can also bake this bread in a springform tin. Roll out the dough and line the greased tin with it. Fill with the sauerkraut mixture and cover with another layer of dough.

Bread in Tins and Flowerpots

These full-flavoured breads with their unusual shapes are ideally suited to the breakfast table, a picnic or even a party buffet

Whole Grain Bread
illustration in foreground

Quantities for 1 25cm/10in tin:

50g/2oz wheat grains
100g/4oz butter
3 eggs
375ml/14 fl oz milk
1 tbsp maple syrup
500g/8oz wholewheat flour
1 packet + 1/4 tsp baking powder
1 tsp sea salt
2 tbsps muesli
Butter for the tin

Preparation time: 30 minutes
Rising time: 12 hours
Baking time: 40 minutes
Nutritional value:
Analysis per slice, if divided into 20 slices, approx:
• 710kJ/170kcal
• 6g protein
• 7g fat
• 20g carbohydrate

Cover the wheat grains with water and leave to soak for 12 hours. • Melt the butter and leave to cool. • Beat the eggs and mix with the butter, milk and syrup. • Rinse the grains in a sieve under cold water and drain well. • Combine the flour, baking powder and salt. Stir the egg mixture into the grains. • Butter the tin and sprinkle with the muesli. • Put the dough in the tin, brush with a little milk, sprinkle with muesli and bake the bread on the centre shelf of a preheated 200°C/400°F/Gas Mark 6 oven for 40 minutes.

Flowerpot Bread
illustration in background

Quantities for 3 12cm/5in high clay flowerpots:

42g/1 1/2oz fresh yeast or
21g/3/4oz dry yeast
1 tbsp sugar
500ml/16 fl oz lukewarm water
300g/10oz wheatmeal flour
250g/8oz wholewheat flour
250g/8oz wholemeal rye flour
3 tsps salt
1 tsp ground coriander
1/2 tsp each of ground caraway seeds and ground fennel
Butter for the flowerpots

Preparation time: 30 minutes
Rising time: 1 3/4 hours
Baking time: 50 minutes
Nutritional value:
Analysis per flowerpot approx:
• 3690kJ/880kcal
• 32g protein
• 4g fat
• 180g carbohydrate

Dissolve the yeast with the sugar in 100ml/4 fl oz lukewarm water. Cover and leave to froth for 15 minutes. • Mix all the flours together and add the yeast mixture, the remaining water, the salt and the spices and knead well. Cover and leave to rise for 1 hour. • Butter the flowerpots and block the hole in the base with aluminium foil. • Knead the dough well again, divide into 3 portions, fill the 3 flowerpots, cover and leave to rise for 30 minutes. • Place an ovenproof dish of cold water in the base of the oven. • Bake the bread in a preheated 230°C/450°F/Gas Mark 8 oven for 40 minutes on the bottom shelf. After 10 minutes, remove the dish of water and reduce the temperature to 200°C/400°F/Gas Mark 6. • Remove the bread from the flowerpots, switch off the oven and return the bread to the oven for 10 minutes.

Flatbreads from the Orient

These exotic flatbreads are broken, not sliced. Perfect accompaniments to a Turkish kebab or Indian curry.

Turkish Flatbreads

illustrated rear

Quantities for 2 flatbreads:

500g/1lb 2oz strong plain flour
1 packet dry yeast
1 tsp salt
1 tsp sugar
100ml/4 fl oz olive oil
250ml/9 fl oz lukewarm water
2 tbsps sesame seeds
Oil for the baking sheet

Preparation time: 30 minutes
Rising time: 1 hour
Baking time: 15-20 minutes
Nutritional value:
Analysis per flatbread, approx:
- 5880kJ/1400kcal
- 29g protein
- 57g fat
- 180g carbohydrate

Combine the flour, dry yeast, salt, sugar and oil. • Slowly add the water. Knead the dough until it is smooth and shiny and leaves the bowl clean. Cover and leave to rise in a warm place for 45 minutes. • Knead the dough well on a lightly floured work surface, shape into 2 balls and roll each out to an oval 1cm/^{1}/$_{2}$in thick. • Place the flatbreads on the greased baking sheet, cover and leave to rise for 15 minutes. • Brush the flatbreads with water, prick all over with a fork, sprinkle with the sesame seeds and bake in the centre of a preheated 250°C/480°F/Gas Mark 10 oven for 15-20 minutes until honey-coloured.

Indian Flatbreads

illustrated front

Quantities for 10 small flatbreads:

500g/1lb 2oz floury potatoes
2 medium onions
1 tbsp butter or vegetable ghee
1 bunch of parsley
600g/1lb 5oz wheatmeal flour
^{1}/$_{2}$ tsp ground cumin
Pinch of cayènne pepper
1 tsp salt
3 tbsps sunflower oil
250ml/9 fl oz water
100g/4oz clarified butter or vegetable ghee

Preparation time: 1 hour
Baking time: 1^{1}/$_{4}$ hours
Nutritional value:
Analysis per flatbread, approx:
- 1680kJ/400kcal
- 10g protein
- 13g fat
- 64g carbohydrate

Boil the potatoes for 30-35 minutes until cooked; peel and mash while still hot. • Chop and fry the onion in the butter until translucent. • Chop the parsley and combine with the mashed potato, flour, spices, salt and oil. Slowly add the water and then add the cooled onion. • Divide the dough into 12 equal portions and roll out into rounds 15cm/6in in diameter on a lightly floured work surface. • Fry the flatbreads in the clarified butter or ghee in a frying pan over a medium heat for 5 minutes on each side. • Keep the flatbreads warm by covering with aluminium foil and placing in a preheated 75°C/170°F oven until they are all cooked. Serve hot with meat or fish.

Swedish Crispbreads

This bread is delicious served with a fish spread, such as salmon, kipper or anchovy paste

Quantities for 10 flatbreads:

350g/11oz wholewheat flour
150g/5½oz wholemeal rye flour
42g/1½oz fresh yeast or
21g/¾oz dry yeast
Pinch of sugar
250ml/9 fl oz lukewarm water
2 tbsps sunflower seeds
2 tsps salt
1 tsp ground caraway seeds
½ tsp ground coriander
2 tbsps sunflower oil
Oil for the baking sheet

Preparation time: 30 minutes
Rising time: 1¼ hours
Baking time per baking sheet: 5-7 minutes
Nutritional value:
Analysis per flatbread, approx:
• 580kJ/210kcal
• 7g protein
• 5g fat
• 33g carbohydrate

Mix all the flour in a bowl and make a well in the centre. Crumble in the fresh yeast, sprinkle with the sugar, mix with the water and a little flour. If using dry yeast, blend the yeast with the sugar, honey, water and a little flour and then pour into the well. Cover and leave to rise in a warm place. • Chop the sunflower seeds finely and add to the flour in the bowl, together with the salt, spices and oil. Mix well. Knead thoroughly until the dough is smooth and elastic and leaves the bowl clean. Cover with a cloth and leave to rise in a warm place for 45 minutes. • Knead the dough well again, turn out onto a floured surface and roll out thinly. Cut into 15x15cm/6x6in squares. • Place the squares on the oiled baking sheet, cover and leave to rise for 15 minutes before baking for 5-7 minutes on the centre shelf of a preheated 250°C/480°F/Gas Mark 10 oven. After 5 minutes in the oven the bread will still be soft – leave it for 7 minutes and it will crispen.

French Bread

The baguette or French bread is everyone's favourite; the secret is in the slow rising

Quantities for 5 French loaves:

1kg/2¹/₂lbs strong plain flour

42g/1¹/₂oz fresh yeast or
21g/³/₄oz dry yeast

Pinch of sugar

750ml/1¹/₄ pints lukewarm water

3 tsps salt

¹/₂ tsp ground aniseed (optional)

Flour for the baking sheet

Preparation time: 30 minutes
Rising time: 1¹/₂ hours
Baking time: 45 minutes
Nutritional value:
Analysis per loaf, approx:
• 2890kJ/690kcal
• 22g protein
• 2g fat
• 150g carbohydrate

Sift the flour into a warmed bowl, make a well in the centre and crumble the fresh yeast into it. Sprinkle the sugar on top and mix in the water and a little flour. If using dry yeast, blend the yeast with the sugar and water and a little flour before pouring into the well. • Sprinkle a little flour over the starter dough, cover and leave to rise in a warm place at about 22°C/70°F for 15 minutes or until cracks appear in the flour. Add the salt and aniseed, if using, and knead all the ingredients until the dough is smooth and elastic. Cover and leave to rise in a warm place for 1 hour or until doubled in bulk. • Dust the baking sheets with flour. • Knead the dough again on a lightly floured surface and divide into 5 equal portions. • Roll each into a 50cm/20in French stick, place on the baking sheet, cover and leave to rise for a further 15 minutes. • Brush the loaves with lukewarm water, make 5 ¹/₂cm/¹/₄in deep diagonal cuts in each loaf and bake on the centre shelf of a preheated 220°C/425°F/Gas Mark 7 oven for 45 minutes until golden-brown. • Baguettes should be served straight from the oven.

Our Tip: If the risen dough is left in a bowl, covered in clingfilm, overnight, you can shape and bake the bread first thing in the morning.

Flatbreads for Every Occasion

Whether baked in the oven or on a griddle, these breads are at their best when very fresh

Garlic Flatbreads
illustrated left

Quantities for 16 flatbreads:

4 garlic cloves

350g/11oz wholewheat flour

150g/5 $^{1}/_{2}$oz gram flour

2 tsps salt

$^{1}/_{2}$ tsp white pepper

1 tsp ground cumin

$^{1}/_{2}$ tsp ground cardamom

200ml/7 fl oz lukewarm water

Preparation time: 20 minutes
Rising time: 8 hours
Baking time: 1 hour
Nutritional value:
Analysis per flatbread, approx:
• 420kJ/100kcal
• 4g protein
• 1g fat
• 22g carbohydrate

Crush the garlic cloves. Place in a bowl and mix with the flours, salt and spices. Add the buttermilk and water gradually, knead the dough well, shape into a ball, wrap it in clingfilm and leave to rise at room temperature for 8 hours. • Knead the dough thoroughly again and divide into 16 equal portions. Shape each slice into a ball, place on a lightly floured surface and roll into a 1cm/$^{1}/_{2}$in thick round. Cook the flatbreads in a dry frying pan or a griddle over a medium to low heat until brown on both sides and then keep them warm in a preheated 75°C/170°F oven until all the flatbreads are ready. • These flatbreads are especially suitable for serving with Indian dishes.

Finnish Flatbreads
illustrated right

Quantities for 8 flatbreads:

350g/11oz wholewheat flour

150g/5$^{1}/_{2}$oz wholemeal rye flour

42g/1$^{1}/_{2}$oz fresh yeast or
21g/$^{1}/_{2}$oz dry yeast

$^{1}/_{2}$ tsp sugar

372ml/14 fl oz lukewarm water

1 tsp salt

4 tbsps oil

FOR THE DECORATION:

Coarse salt, poppy seeds or sesame seeds

Greaseproof paper for the baking sheet

Preparation time: 30 minutes
Rising time: 1$^{1}/_{2}$ hours
Baking time: 20 minutes
Nutritional value:
Analysis per flatbread, approx:
• 420kJ/100kcal
• 4g protein
• 6g fat
• 39g carbohydrate

Mix the flours, make a well in the centre, crumble the fresh yeast into it and sprinkle with the sugar. Mix half the water and a little flour with the yeast. If using dry yeast, blend the yeast with the sugar, half the water and a little flour and pour it into the well. Cover and leave to rise in a warm place for 15 minutes. Then mix in all the flour, salt, remaining water, 2 tsps oil and knead thoroughly. Shape the dough into a ball, cover and leave to rise for 1 hour. • Line the baking sheet with greaseproof paper. • Knead the dough well, shape into 8 balls and roll each ball out to a 1cm/$^{1}/_{2}$in thick round. Place the rounds on the baking sheet, prick with a fork, brush with the remaining oil and sprinkle with the coarse salt, poppy seeds or sesame seeds. Cover and leave to rise again for 30 minutes. • Bake on the centre shelf of a preheated 220°C/425°F/Gas Mark 7 oven for 20 minutes.

Onion Bread

This delicious Viennese bread should ideally be baked in a round bread or biscuit tin. It is traditionally served with new white wine.

Quantities for 1 20-24cm/8-10in diameter round bread tin:

400g/14oz wholewheat flour
100g/4oz rye flour
1 tbsp caraway seeds
Pinch of black pepper
2 tsps sea salt
42g/1¹/₂oz fresh yeast or 21g/³/₄oz dry yeast
2 tsps clear honey
250g/8oz sour cream
100ml/4 fl oz hot water
250g/8oz onions
4 tbsps sunflower oil
Butter for the tin

Preparation time: 30 minutes
Rising time: 1 hour
Baking time: 45-55 minutes
Nutritional value:
Analysis per slice, if divided into 25 slices, approx:
- 375kJ/90kcal
- 3g protein
- 3g fat
- 13g carbohydrate

Combine the wheat and rye flours with the caraway seeds, pepper and salt in a mixing bowl. • Make a well in the centre of the flour, crumble in the fresh yeast, pour over the honey and wait 2 minutes for the yeast to dissolve. • Mix the sour cream with the hot water, pour this over the yeast and stir, incorporating a little flour from around the edge. If using dry yeast, add the yeast and the honey to the sour cream and water and pour into the well in the flour. Sprinkle a little flour on top of the starter dough, cover and leave to rise in a warm place at about 22°C/70°F for roughly 20 minutes until cracks appear in the flour. • Chop the onions finely and fry in the oil until golden-brown. • Mix all the flour with the starter dough and then knead well. • Cover the dough again and leave to rise for about 20 minutes. • Knead the dough thoroughly once more and incorporate the cooled onions and

the fat from the frying pan. If the dough is too firm, add a little more water; if it is too soft and does not leave the bowl clean, add a little more wholewheat flour. • Butter the bread tin. • Turn the dough out on to a lightly floured work surface, shape into a ball, place in the tin and press down gently. • Leave the dough to rise again for 20 minutes until it has increased in bulk by one-third. • Place the tin in the centre of a preheated 200°C/400°F/Gas Mark 6 oven and bake for 45-55 minutes until golden-brown. • Take the bread out of the tin, place on a wire rack and brush or spray all over with a little cold water and leave to cool. • This bread is delicious straight from the oven.

Our Tip: If you do not have a round bread tin, you can use a suitable size of ovenproof cast iron or stainless steel pan or casserole. Alternatively, simply shape the dough into an oblong and bake on a buttered baking sheet. If you choose this option, reduce the baking time by 10 minutes.

Golden Plaits

Delicious for breakfast with butter and jam

Quantities for 2 plaits:

21g/³/₄oz fresh yeast or 10g/¹/₄oz dry yeast
1 tbsp sugar
600ml/1 pint lukewarm milk
1kg/2¹/₄lbs strong plain white flour
2 tsps salt
100g/4oz soft butter
2 tbsps condensed milk
Butter for the baking sheet

Preparation time: 40 minutes
Rising time: 1³/₄ hours
Baking time: 40 minutes
Nutritional value:
Analysis per slice, if divided into 30 slices, approx:
- 630kJ/150kcal
- 4g protein
- 4g fat
- 25g carbohydrate

Blend the yeast and sugar with 125ml/4 fl oz milk. Cover and leave to froth in a warm place for 15 minutes. Add the yeast mixture to the flour, the remaining milk, salt and butter and knead to a workable dough.
- Cover and leave to rise in a warm place for 1 hour. • Knead the dough again and divide into 6 portions. Place on a lightly floured surface and shape each portion into a 50cm/20in long strip. Lay 3 strips together and make into a plait. Repeat for the second plait. Butter the baking sheet, place the plaits on it, cover and leave to rise for 30 minutes. • Place an ovenproof dish of cold water on the floor of the oven. • Brush the plaits with the condensed milk and bake on the centre shelf of a preheated 200°C/400°F/Gas Mark 6 oven for 40 minutes. Remove the dish of water from the oven after 10 minutes. • Cool the plaits on a wire rack and serve very fresh.

Our Tip: For a more intricate plait, use 4 strips of dough.

Sweet Yeast Bread

Freshly baked and served with butter and honey, this bread is as good as any cake

Quantities for 1 loaf:

42g/1¹/₂oz fresh yeast or
21g/³/₄oz dry yeast
1 tbsp sugar
200ml/7 fl oz lukewarm milk
100g/4oz currants
4 tbsps rum
650g/1lb 7oz strong, plain white flour
75g/3oz butter
100g/4oz sugar
1 egg
Pinch of salt
100g/4oz chopped hazelnuts
3 tbsps milk
Butter for the tin

Preparation time: 40 minutes
Rising time: 2¹/₄ hours
Baking time: 25-30 minutes
Nutritional value:
Analysis per slice, if divided into 40 slices, approx:
• 460kJ/110kcal
• 3g protein
• 4g fat
• 17g carbohydrate

Dissolve the yeast and sugar in 100ml/4 fl oz milk, cover and leave in a warm place to froth. • Wash the currants in hot water, pat them dry and soak them in the rum. • Mix the flour with the yeast mixture and the remaining milk. • Melt the butter and add to the dough together with the sugar, egg, salt, hazelnuts, currants and rum. Knead well until the dough leaves the bowl clean. • Cover and leave the dough to rise in a warm place for 1¹/₂ hours. • Butter the baking sheet. • Knead the dough again and divide it into 2 portions. Place them on a lightly floured work surface and roll each into a 50cm/20in strip. Twist the strips of dough around each other in a spiral formation and place on the baking sheet. • Cover and leave to rise for another 30 minutes. • Place an ovenproof dish of cold water in the base of the oven. • Brush the dough with the milk and bake in the centre of a preheated 220°C/425°F/Gas Mark 7 oven for 25-30 minutes. • After 10 minutes remove the dish of water from the oven and reduce the temperature to 200°C/400°F/Gas Mark 6.

Greek Easter Bread

A traditional delicacy which is worth eating all year round

Quantities for 1 loaf:

600g/1lb 5oz strong plain flour

42g/1½oz fresh yeast or 21g/¾oz dry yeast

100g/4oz sugar

7 tbsps lukewarm water

Pinch of salt

Zest of one lemon

50g/2oz candied lemon peel, finely chopped

½ tsp ground aniseed

125g/5oz soft butter

7 tbsps lukewarm water

5 hard-boiled eggs painted with red food colouring

Olive oil • 1 egg yolk

2 tbsps sesame seeds

Butter for the baking sheet

Preparation time: 45 minutes
Rising time: 3½ – 4½ hours
Baking time: 40-45 minutes
Nutritional value:
Analysis per slice, if divided into 20 slices, not including the eggs:
• 880kJ/210kcal
• 5g protein
• 10g fat
• 29g carbohydrate

If using fresh yeast, crumble the yeast and mix it with 125g/5 oz of the flour, 1 tsp sugar and the water. If using dry yeast, blend the yeast with 1 tsp sugar, the water and 125g/5 oz of the flour; make a well in the centre of the rest of the flour and pour the yeast mixture into it. Leave to rise for 15 minutes. • Add the other ingredients up to and including the milk; knead the dough well and leave to rise for 3-4 hours. • Knead the dough thoroughly again and divide into 3 equal portions and 1 larger portion; shape these into strips. Make the three equal strips into a plait; place the thicker strip on top and press down gently. • Make little hollows in the dough for the eggs. Rub the eggs with oil and press into the plait. • Cover and leave to prove for 20 minutes. • Brush the plait with the beaten egg, sprinkle with the sesame seeds and bake in a preheated 180°C/350°F/Gas Mark 4 oven for 40-45 minutes.

Swedish Christmas Bread

Lemon zest can be substituted for bitter orange peel when Seville oranges are not in season

Quantities for 1 wide, 30cm/12in tin of 2.5l/4½ pint capacity:

750g/1lb 11oz wholemeal rye flour

500g/1lb 2oz wholewheat flour

60g/2oz fresh yeast or 30g/1oz dry yeast

500ml/18 fl oz buttermilk

50g/2oz golden syrup

½ tsp salt

2 tsps grated Seville orange peel

¼ tsp each cardamom and coriander seeds, crushed

50g/2oz raisins

2 tbsps golden syrup

Butter for the tin

Preparation time: 30 minutes
Rising time: 2 hours
Baking time: 30 minutes
Nutritional value:
Analysis per slice, if divided into 40 slices, approx:
• 545kJ/130kcal
• 4g protein
• 1g fat
• 26g carbohydrate

Mix the flours together in a large bowl and make a well in the centre. Crumble the fresh yeast into the well • Warm the butter, milk and syrup, stirring constantly. Mix about 250ml/9 fl oz of this mixture with the yeast and a little flour. If using dry yeast, blend the yeast with 250ml/9 fl oz of the liquid before pouring it into the well and mixing with a little flour. • Cover the starter dough and leave it to rise for 15 minutes. • Add the salt, spices and remaining buttermilk to the flour and starter dough and knead thoroughly until the dough leaves the bowl clean. Cover and leave to rise for 1 hour. • Wash the raisins in hot water and pat dry. • Knead the dough again and incorporate the raisins. Butter the tin, place the dough in it, cover loosely and leave to rise until doubled in volume. • Heat the syrup with 1 tbsp water. • Cut the top of the dough in a grid pattern, brush with the syrup and bake on a low shelf in a preheated 220°C/425°F/Gas Mark 7 oven for 50 minutes.

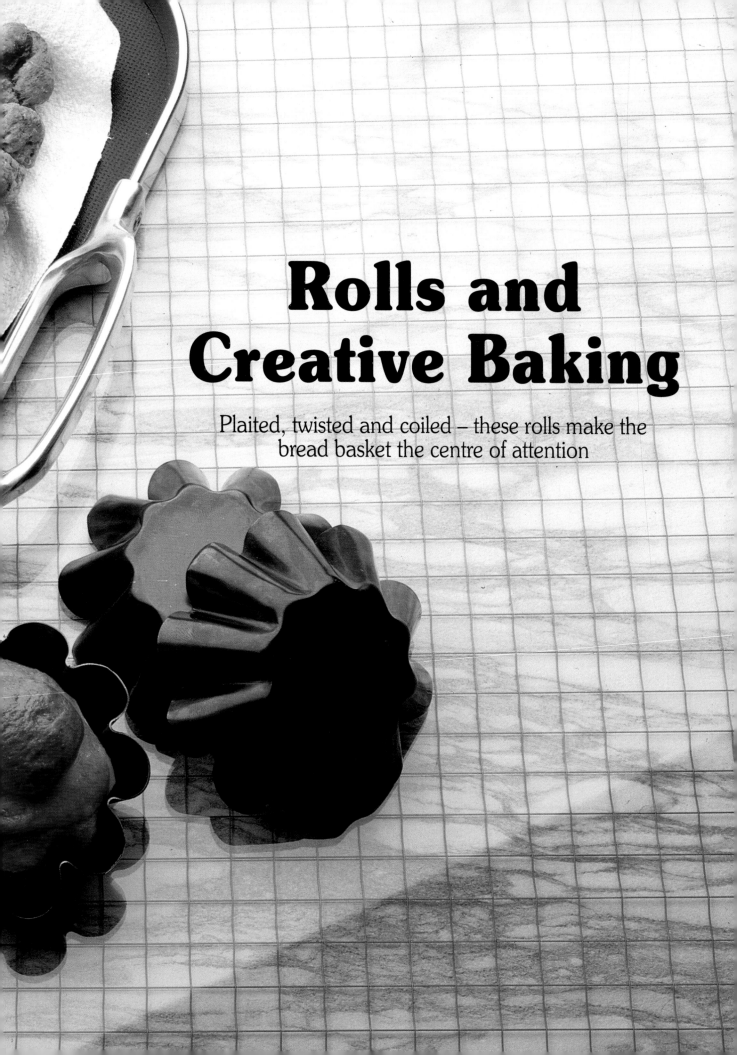

Rolls and Creative Baking

Plaited, twisted and coiled – these rolls make the
bread basket the centre of attention

Buckwheat Rolls

As a tasty alternative to pumpkin seeds, try these rolls with walnuts

Sesame Rye Rolls

Even after two days these rolls taste as if they've been freshly baked

Quantities for 10 rolls:

250g/8oz wholewheat flour	
250g/8oz buckwheat flour	
42g/1¹/₂oz fresh yeast or	
21g/³/₄oz dry yeast	
500ml/16 fl oz lukewarm buttermilk	
Pinch of sugar	
1 tsp sea salt	
50g/2oz pumpkin seeds	
Butter for the baking sheet	

Preparation time: 40 minutes
Rising time: 1¹/₂ hours
Baking time: 25 minutes
Nutritional value:
Analysis per roll, approx:
• 880kJ/210kcal
• 8g protein
• 3g fat
• 36g carbohydrate

Measure the flours into a bowl, make a well in the centre, crumble in the fresh yeast and stir with a little buttermilk, the sugar and a little of the flours. If using dry yeast, blend the yeast with the buttermilk and sugar, and add to the flour. • Cover and leave to rise in a warm place for 15 minutes. • Add the remaining buttermilk and salt to the starter dough and knead these together with the remaining flour to form a soft, smooth dough. • Cover and leave to rise for 1 hour. • Set aside 1 tbsp of the pumpkin seeds and chop the rest finely. • Knead the pumpkin seeds into the dough and shape it into 10 equal-sized balls. • Butter the baking sheet. Place the rolls on the baking sheet, cover and leave to rise for a further 15 minutes. • Make deep crosses in the rolls with a wet knife, brush them with cold water, and sprinkle with the remaining pumpkin seeds, pressing them down gently. • Bake the rolls on the centre shelf of a preheated 220°C/425°F/Gas Mark 7 oven for 25 minutes or until golden-brown.

Quantities for 14 rolls:

500g/1lb 2oz wholemeal rye flour	
250g/8oz wholewheat flour	
42g/1¹/₂oz fresh yeast or	
21g/³/₄oz dry yeast	
600ml/18 fl oz lukewarm water	
Pinch of sugar	
1 tbsp sea salt	
Pinch each of white pepper and freshly grated nutmeg	
150g/5¹/₂oz sourdough	

FOR THE DECORATION:

3 tbsps raw sesame seeds	
Butter for the baking sheet	

Preparation time: 20 minutes
Rising time: 1³/₄ hours
Baking time: 25 minutes
Nutritional value:
Analysis per roll, approx:
• 880kJ/210kcal
• 8g protein
• 2g fat
• 39g carbohydrate

Mix the flours in a bowl. Make a well in the centre, crumble in the fresh yeast, mix in 100ml/3 fl oz of the water, the sugar and a little flour. If using dry yeast, blend the yeast with the water and sugar and then pour over the flour. • Cover and leave to rise in a warm place for 15 minutes. • Knead the remaining flour into the starter dough, add the remaining water, salt, spices and sourdough and work into a smooth dough. Cover and leave to rise until it has doubled in volume – this will take approximately 1 hour. • Grease the baking sheet with butter. • Knead the dough again thoroughly and shape into 14 equal-sized balls. Press down firmly to make them flattish, lay them on the baking sheet and cover. Leave to prove for 30 minutes. • Brush the rolls with cold water, make a shallow cross on the top of each, sprinkle with the sesame seeds and press them in gently. • Bake the rolls on the centre shelf of a preheated 220°C/425°F/Gas Mark 7 oven for about 25 minutes or until golden-brown.

Creative Party Rolls

These attractively shaped rolls are particularly popular with guests

Quantities for 19 rolls:

800g/1lb 12oz wholewheat flour

200g/7oz wheatmeal flour

750ml/26 fl oz lukewarm water

4 tsps dry yeast

1 tsp sugar

1 tbsp salt

Pinch each of ground coriander and cardamom

FOR THE DECORATION:

3 tbsps each of poppy seeds and sesame seeds

Greaseproof paper for the baking sheet

Preparation time: 1¼ hours

Rising time: 14 hours

Baking time: 35 minutes

Nutritional value:

Analysis per roll, approx:

- 750kJ/180kcal
- 7g protein
- 3g fat
- 33g carbohydrate

Mix the flours in a large bowl and make a well in the centre. • Add the sourdough to the well, mix it with a little water and sprinkle with the sugar and dry yeast. • Sprinkle the salt and spices onto the edge of the flour. Mix all the flours with the remaining water and stir into the sourdough mixture; knead it until the dough is elastic and smooth. • Shape the dough into a ball, dust with flour and cover with a cloth. Leave to rise in a warm place for 3 hours. • Knead the dough thoroughly again; if it is still a little sticky, incorporate a little more wholewheat flour. • Line the baking sheet with greaseproof paper. • On a lightly floured work surface, shape the dough into a long roll about 7cm/3in in diameter. Cut the roll into 13 equal-sized pieces. • Make one round roll and place in the centre of the baking sheet. • Roll the remaining dough into sausage shapes, about 15cm/6in in length.

Mould half of them into rings; press the ends together gently and lay them round the centre roll. Form the other six sausages into crescent shapes and place in an outer circle, so that they join the rings together. They should just touch one another. • Cover the rolls with a cloth and leave to rise for a further 2 hours. • Brush the risen rolls with lukewarm water. Decorate the centre roll and crescent shapes with poppy seeds; sprinkle sesame seeds onto the rings. • Bake the rolls on the centre shelf of a preheated 220°C/425°F/Gas Mark 7 oven for 15 minutes. Reduce the temperature to 180°C/350°F/Gas Mark 4 and bake for a further 20 minutes until golden-brown. • Leave the rolls to cool on the baking sheet for a few minutes, then slide carefully onto a wire rack. • Serve fresh from the oven.

Our Tip: If your baking sheet is too small for this quantity of rolls,

divide the dough into 2 pieces and bake two batches, one after the other. If you have neither the time nor inclination to bake the batch as described above, form small, round rolls from the risen dough and arrange them in two 24cm/9 ½in diameter springform tins, spreading out from the centre. Sprinkle some with poppy seeds and some with sesame seeds, and bake at the same temperature as the rolls in the main recipe for 45 minutes.

Tangy Aniseed Rolls

A pleasant change for the breakfast table

Crispy Bacon Crowns

As an alternative to caraway, try decorating the rolls with poppy seeds

Tangy Aniseed Rolls

Quantities for 12 rolls:

500g/1lb 2oz wheatmeal flour	
1 packet dry yeast	
Pinch of sugar	
1 tsp salt	
1 tsp ground aniseed	
250ml/9 fl oz lukewarm milk	
100g/4oz softened butter	
1 egg	
1 tbsp condensed milk	
1 tbsp each of peeled, chopped almonds and pistachios	
Butter for the baking sheet	

Preparation time: 20 minutes
Rising time: 1 hour
Baking time: 20-25 minutes
Nutritional value:
Analysis per roll, approx:
• 1000kJ/240kcal
• 7g protein
• 10g fat
• 32g carbohydrate

Combine the flour in a bowl with the yeast, sugar, salt and aniseed. • Add the milk, butter and egg and knead together to form a smooth dough. • Dust the dough with flour and cover. Leave to rise in a warm place for 45 minutes. • Butter the baking sheet. • Knead the dough again, shape into a roll and divide into 12 equal-sized pieces. • Shape the pieces into rolls, lay them on the baking sheet and cover. Leave to rise for a further 15 minutes. • Brush the rolls with the condensed milk; decorate six with the chopped almonds and the rest with the chopped pistachios. Bake the aniseed rolls on the centre shelf of a preheated 200°C/400°F/Gas Mark 6 oven for 20 to 25 minutes until golden.

Crispy Bacon Crowns

Quantities for 12 rolls:

500g/1lb 2oz wheatmeal flour	
1 packet dry yeast	
Pinch of sugar	
1/2 tsp salt	
250ml/9 fl oz lukewarm milk	
100g/4oz softened butter	
1 egg	
1 onion	
200g/7oz rindless streaky bacon rashers	
1/2 tsp dried thyme	
1 tbsp condensed milk	
1 tsp caraway seeds	
Butter for the baking sheet	

Preparation time: 30 minutes
Rising time: 1 hour
Baking time: 20 minutes
Nutritional value:
Analysis per roll, approx: •
1380kJ/330kcal
• 8g protein
• 20g fat
• 32g carbohydrate

Mix the flour with the yeast, sugar and salt. • Add the milk, butter and egg; knead everything together thoroughly. Cover and leave to rise in a warm place for 45 minutes. • Peel the onions and dice finely. • Cut the bacon into narrow strips and dry fry until the fat begins to run. Add the onion cubes and fry for 2 minutes, then add the crushed thyme. Leave to cool. • Butter the baking sheet. • Knead the dough again, divide into 12 equal-sized pieces, spread them out flat and place the bacon mixture on top. Bring the edges of the dough up round the filling and press firmly. • Arrange the rolls on the baking sheet smooth side up, cover and leave to rise for 15 minutes. • Now make a cross in the top of each roll, brush with condensed milk, sprinkle with the caraway seeds and bake in a preheated 200°C/400°F/Gas Mark 6 oven for 20 minutes.

Yeast Crescents

These light crescents should be served fresh from the oven, with either sweet or savoury accompaniments

Quantities for 16 crescents:

42g/1½oz fresh yeast or 21g/¾oz dry yeast
1 tbsp sugar
300ml/12 fl oz lukewarm water
750g/1lb 11oz wheatmeal flour
2 tsps salt
3 tbsps condensed milk
Butter for the baking sheet

Preparation time: 30 minutes
Rising time: 2 hours
Baking time: 30 minutes
Nutritional value:
Analysis per crescent, approx:
• 710kJ/170kcal
• 6g protein
• 1g fat
• 36g carbohydrate

Dissolve the crumbled fresh yeast or dry yeast with the sugar in 5 tbsps of lukewarm water, cover and leave to rise for 15 minutes in a warm place, at about 22°C/70°F. • Stir the flour, remaining lukewarm water and salt into the yeast mixture and knead thoroughly, until the dough leaves the bowl clean. • Cover and leave to rise in a warm place for another hour. • Knead the dough thoroughly again and divide into 2 portions. • On a lightly floured work surface roll each portion out into a circle about 40cm/16in in diameter. Cut the circle into 8 equal-sized triangles, as for a cake. • Butter the baking sheet. • Cut a slit of about 5cm/2in in the centre of the base of each of the dough triangles . Roll the triangles up from the base to the tip, mould into crescents and place on the baking sheet. • Cover and leave to rise for 45 minutes. • Stand an ovenproof bowl containing cold water in the base of the oven. • Brush the crescents with condensed milk and bake on the centre shelf of a preheated 225°C/430°F/Gas Mark 7 oven for 30 minutes until golden-brown. After 10 minutes, remove the water from the oven and lower the temperature to 200°C/400°F/Gas Mark 6.

Wheatmeal or Cornmeal Muffins

Bake these in American muffin tins, English patty pans, or individual foil muffin cups

Wheatmeal Muffins
illustrated rear

Quantities for 1 12-cup muffin tin or 12 individual foil cups:

300g/10oz wheatmeal flour
20g/³/₄oz sugar
2 tsps baking powder
¹/₂ tsp salt
1 egg
125ml/4 fl oz milk
6 tbsps salad oil
1 tbsp sesame seeds
1 tbsp chopped pumpkin seeds
Oil for the tin or cups

Preparation time: 20 minutes
Baking time: 20-25 minutes
Nutritional value:
Analysis per muffin, approx:
- 670kJ/160kcal
- 4g protein
- 6g fat
- 22g carbohydrate

Brush the muffin sheet or aluminium tins lightly with oil. • Combine the flour, sugar, baking powder and salt in a bowl. • Add the egg, milk and oil and stir to form a thick dough. • Spoon the dough into the muffin tin or aluminium cups and sprinkle alternately with sesame seeds and pumpkin seeds. • Bake the muffins on the centre shelf of a preheated 200°C/400°F/Gas Mark 6 oven for 20 to 25 minutes or until golden. • Leave to cool on a wire rack and serve as soon as possible after baking.

Cornmeal Muffins
illustrated front

Quantities for 10 cups :

250ml/9 fl oz milk
220g/7oz fine yellow cornmeal
50g/2oz wheatmeal flour
2 tsps baking powder
1 tsp salt
¹/₂ tsp ground aniseed
1 tbsp sugar
2 eggs
50g/2oz soft butter
Butter and dry breadcrumbs for the tins

Preparation time: 20 minutes
Rising time: 10 minutes
Baking time: 20-30 minutes
Nutritional value:
Analysis per muffin, approx:
- 755kJ/180 kcal
- 6g protein
- 8g fat
- 22g carbohydrate

Butter the tins and sprinkle them evenly with breadcrumbs, shaking off the excess. • Bring the milk to the boil. Place the cornmeal in a bowl, pour the boiling milk over it, cover and leave to steep for 10 minutes. • Mix the flour with the baking powder and add to the cornmeal mixture with the salt, aniseed and sugar. Stir in the eggs and butter. • Spoon the dough into the cups. Bake the muffins on the centre shelf of a preheated 200°C/400°F/Gas Mark 6 oven for 20 to 30 minutes or until golden-brown. • Cornmeal muffins are at their best when still warm, generously spread with chilled butter.

Pepper Plaits

As a variation, try using 1 courgette and 1 garlic clove instead of peppers

Quantities for 4 plaits:

500g/1lb 2oz wheatmeal flour
1 packet dry yeast
1 tsp salt
1/2 tsp sugar
250ml/9 fl oz lukewarm milk
2 tbsps sour cream
40g/1¹/₂oz soft butter
1 green pepper
1 red pepper
1 chilli
1 medium sized onion
2 tbsps oil
1 egg yolk
2 tbsps sesame seeds
Butter for the baking sheet

Preparation time: 40 minutes
Rising time: 1 hour
Baking time: 30 minutes
Nutritional value:
Analysis per plait, approx:
• 3400kJ/810 kcal
• 23g protein
• 27g fat
• 99g carbohydrate

Mix the flour with the yeast, salt and sugar. • Add the milk, sour cream and butter, and knead them together thoroughly. • Cover and leave to rise for 30 minutes. • Deseed the peppers and chilli; dice finely. • Peel and finely chop the onions. • Heat the oil, fry the vegetables for 3 minutes and leave to cool. • Knead the dough again and incorporate the vegetables. • Butter the baking sheet. • Divide the dough into 4 portions and form three equal-sized rolls from each piece. Weave them together to form 4 plaits, lay them on the baking sheet, cover and leave to rise for 30 minutes. • Beat the egg yolk with 1 tbsp water. Brush the plaits with the egg mixture, sprinkle with the sesame seeds and bake on the centre shelf of a preheated 200°C/400°F/Gas Mark 6 oven for about 30 minutes until golden-brown.

Caraway Seed Rolls

Make these with wholemeal flour only for an even bolder flavour

Quantities for 25 rolls:

63g/2oz fresh yeast or
32g/1oz dry yeast
600ml/18 fl oz lukewarm water
2 tbsps sugar
450g/1lb wholewheat flour
450g/1lb wheatmeal flour
2 tsps salt
6 tbsps caraway seeds
Butter for the baking sheet

Preparation time: 45 minutes
Rising time: 1¹/₂ hours
Baking time: 20-25 minutes
Nutritional value:
Analysis per roll, approx:
• 545kJ/130kcal
• 4g protein
• 1g fat
• 25g carbohydrate

Dissolve the crumbled fresh yeast or dry yeast with the sugar in 100ml/4 fl oz of the water, cover and leave to froth in a warm place for 15 minutes. • Combine the flours and stir in the remaining lukewarm water, salt and yeast mixture; knead thoroughly until the dough leaves the bowl clean. • Cover and leave to rise in a warm place for 1 hour. • Butter the baking sheet. • Add 2 tbsps of the caraway seeds to the dough and knead thoroughly again. Divide the dough into 25 equal-sized pieces and shape into balls. • Press down firmly to make them round and flattish; with a floured finger make a hole in the middle and roll the dough round your finger to make a ring. • Lay the rings on the baking sheet, cover and leave to rise for 15 minutes. • Cut deep crosses in the surface of the rings, brush them with water and sprinkle with the remaining caraway seeds, pressing them in gently. • Place a cup of cold water in the base of the oven and preheat it to 220°C/425°F/Gas Mark 7 . Bake the rings for 5 minutes, then reduce the temperature to 200°C/400°F/Gas Mark 6 and bake for a further 15 to 20 minutes.

Party Batch

Your guests will be delighted by these delicious, quick-and-easy rolls

Quantities for 2 batches (20 rolls in each):

1kg/2¼lbs strong plain flour	
42g/1½oz fresh yeast or 21g/¾oz dry yeast	
1 tsp sugar	
500ml/16fl oz lukewarm water	
2 tsps salt	

FOR THE DECORATION AND GLAZE:

125ml/4 fl oz milk	
3 tbsps pumpkin seeds	
3 tbsps raw peanuts	
3 tbsps sesame seeds	
2 tbsps coarse salt	
Butter for the baking sheet	

Preparation time: 1 hour
Rising time: 2 hours
Baking time (per batch): 20 minutes
Nutritional value:

Analysis per roll, approx:
• 420kJ/100kcal
• 3g protein
• 2g fat
• 19g carbohydrate

Sift the flour into a bowl and make a well in the centre. Crumble in the fresh yeast, add the sugar, 8 tbsps of water and a little of the flour, and stir to form a dough. If using dry yeast, blend the yeast with the sugar and water and then add to the flour. • Dust the dough with a little flour, cover with a cloth and leave to rise in a warm place (about 22°C/70°F), until fine cracks appear on the surface of the flour – this should take about 20 minutes. • Take the starter dough, mix it with the remaining flour and lukewarm water, and the salt, and knead into a light, elastic dough which leaves the bowl clean. • Brush the surface of the dough with a little water, cover and leave to rise in a warm place for a further 45 minutes, by which time it should have doubled in bulk. • Now knead the dough thoroughly again and leave to rise for a further 15 minutes. • Butter two baking sheets. • Shape the dough into two large, equal-sized rolls and cut each roll into 20 equal-sized slices. • Form these into balls and set 20 balls close to each other on each baking sheet. • Chop the pumpkin seeds and peanuts. • Brush the rolls with the milk and decorate them alternately with the pumpkin seeds, peanuts, sesame seeds and coarse salt. • Cover each batch with a cloth and leave to rise in a warm place for 30 minutes. • Bake one after the other, on the centre shelf of a preheated 200°C/400°F/Gas Mark 6 oven for about 20 minutes until golden-brown. • Use a spatula or palette knife to slide them carefully onto a wire rack and leave to cool.

Our Tip: The seeds and nuts used to decorate the rolls can be varied according to individual preference. They also look and taste good with chopped sunflower seeds and poppy seeds, for example, or white poppy seeds and nigella.

Herbed Scones

These are best served straight from the oven

Quantities for 12 scones:

6 tbsps mixed fresh herbs, e.g. cress, marjoram and fresh dill
200g/7oz wheatmeal flour
50g/2oz wholewheat flakes
1 tsp baking powder
1 tsp salt
Pinch of pepper
50g/2oz butter
5 tbsps sour cream or thick-set yogurt
1 egg
Butter for the baking sheet

Preparation time: 30 minutes
Baking time: 15 minutes
Nutritional value:
Analysis per scone, approx:
• 500kJ/120kcal
• 4g protein
• 5g fat
• 13g carbohydrate

Finely chop the herbs. • Butter the baking sheet. • Mix the flour with the wheatflakes, baking powder, salt and pepper. • Cut the butter into cubes and add to the flour. Combine with the sour cream or thick-set yogurt and herbs and knead together. • On a lightly floured work surface roll out the dough to a thickness of roughly 2cm/³/₄in. Cut out 12 circles of about 7cm/2³/₄in diameter and lay them on the baking sheet. • Brush the scones with the beaten egg and bake on the centre shelf of a preheated 225°C/430°F/Gas Mark 7 oven for 15 minutes until golden.

Yeast Crescents

Vary the quantities of wholemeal and refined flour to suit your tastes

Quantities for 16 crescents:

42g/1¹/₂oz fresh yeast or 21g/³/₄oz dry yeast
500ml/16 fl oz lukewarm water
1 tsp sugar
200g/7oz wholewheat flour
600g/1¹/₂lbs wheatmeal flour
2 tsps salt
3 tbsps condensed milk
4 tbsps coarse salt
Butter for the baking sheet

Preparation time: 30 minutes
Rising time: 1³/₄ hours
Baking time: 35 minutes
Nutritional value:
Analysis per crescent, approx:
• 755kJ/180kcal
• 6g protein
• 1g fat
• 35g carbohydrate

Stir the crumbled fresh yeast or dry yeast with the sugar into 100ml/3 fl oz lukewarm water, cover and leave to froth at room temperature for 15 minutes. • Mix the flours with the salt in a bowl and knead thoroughly with the yeast mixture and the remaining water. • Cover and leave to rise for 1 hour. • Knead thoroughly again, roll out to two circles of 40cm/16in diameter and cut each into 8 equal-sized pieces. Roll each triangle out further, and then roll it up towards the pointed tip. • Butter the baking sheet. Lay the crescents on the sheet, cover and leave to rise for 30 minutes. • Set an ovenproof bowl of cold water in the base of the oven. • Brush the crescents with condensed milk, sprinkle with the coarse salt and bake on the centre shelf of a preheated 225°C/430°F/Gas Mark 7 oven for 30 minutes until golden. After 10 minutes remove the water from the oven and lower the temperature to 200°C/400°F/Gas Mark 6. Once the baking time is up, switch off the oven and leave the crescents there for another 5 minutes.

Beer Rolls

Malt beer can be bought at West Indian shops but if it is hard to find, use stout

Quantities for 16 rolls:

500g/1lb 2oz wholewheat flour

100g/4oz rye flour

1/2 tsp each of ground aniseed and caraway seeds

1 tsp sea salt

42g/1 1/2 oz fresh yeast or 21g/3/4 oz dry yeast

1 tbsp golden syrup, treacle or molasses

275ml10 fl oz lukewarm malt beer

Preparation time: 30 minutes
Rising time: 1 hour
Baking time: 20-25 minutes
Nutritional value:
Analysis per roll, approx:
• 500kJ/120kcal
• 4g protein
• 1g fat
• 23g carbohydrate

Combine the wheat and rye flours and mix them in a bowl with the spices and salt. • Make a well in the centre, crumble in the fresh yeast, pour on the syrup and leave for 2 minutes until the yeast has dissolved. If using dry yeast, blend with the syrup and then pour onto the flour. Stir the beer and a little flour into the yeast mixture, cover and leave for 15 minutes at room temperature. • Mix the remaining flour with the starter dough and knead until the flour has absorbed all the liquid. • Cover and leave to rise in a warm place for 30 minutes. • Butter the baking sheet. • Knead the dough again, and add a little water or flour if necessary. • Divide the dough into 16 equal-sized portions, shape into balls and arrange them on the baking sheet. Press them firmly to make them round and flattish. Cover and leave to prove, until the rolls have increased in bulk by about one-third. This will take about 20 minutes. • Bake on the centre shelf of a preheated 200℃/400°F/Gas Mark 6 oven for 20 to 25 minutes until golden-brown. • Spray a little cold water on the rolls and leave to cool on a wire sheet.

Peanut Pinwheels

For lower calorie pinwheels, use almonds or brazil nuts instead of peanuts

Quantities for 15 pinwheels:

300g/10oz strong plain white flour

100g/4oz wheatmeal flour

20g/³/₄oz soya flour

42g/1¹/₂oz fresh yeast or
21g/³/₄oz dry yeast

2 tsps runny honey

250ml/9 fl oz lukewarm buttermilk

1 tsp sea salt

100g/4oz softened butter

100g/4oz unsalted roasted peanuts

1 egg

1 tbsp each of finely chopped
parsley and chives

Pinch of freshly ground black
pepper

Butter for the baking sheet

Preparation time: 45 minutes
Rising time: 1 hour
Baking time: 25 minutes
Nutritional value:
Analysis per pinwheel, approx:
- 710kJ/170kcal
- 7g protein
- 8g fat
- 19g carbohydrate

Combine the wheat flours with the soya flour. Make a well in the centre. • Crumble in the fresh yeast, add the honey and leave for 2 minutes, or until the yeast has dissolved. If using dry yeast, blend the yeast with the honey and then combine with the flour. • Stir the buttermilk into the yeast mixture with a little flour. Cover and leave to rise for 15 minutes at room temperature. • Stir the starter dough into the rest of the flour, add the salt and 50g/2oz of the butter. Knead the dough thoroughly, cover and leave to rise for a further 20 minutes. • Chop the peanuts and melt the remaining butter. • Butter the baking sheet. • Knead the dough thoroughly and roll out to a 30x40cm/12x16in circle. Brush the dough with the melted butter and beaten egg, sprinkle with the peanuts, herbs and pepper, roll up and cut into slices 2cm/³/₄in thick. Arrange the pinwheels on the baking sheet, cover and leave to rise for 25 minutes. • Bake the pinwheels for 20 to 25 minutes in a preheated 200°C/400°F/Gas Mark 6 oven until golden-brown, then spray with a little cold water and leave to cool on a wire rack.

Wholegrain Rolls

Refined flour combinations have long been an essential element of these popular breakfast rolls

Wheatmeal Rolls
illustrated left and right

Quantities for 12 rolls:

350g/11oz wholewheat flour

150g/5½oz fine wheatmeal flour

42g/1½oz fresh yeast or
21g/¾oz dry yeast

1 tsp acacia honey

125ml/4 fl oz each of lukewarm
milk and lukewarm water

Pinch of sea salt

2 pinches each of ground aniseed
and coriander

FOR THE DECORATION:

3 tbsps cracked wheat

Butter for the baking sheet

Preparation time: 30 minutes
Rising time: 1½ hours
Baking time: 25 minutes
Nutritional value:
Analysis per roll, approx:
• 630kJ/150kcal
• 6g protein
• 1g fat
• 28g carbohydrate

Combine the flours and make a well in the centre. Crumble in the fresh yeast and pour the honey over it. If using dry yeast, blend the yeast with the honey and then pour this into the flour. • Mix the milk with the water, pour a little of the liquid onto the yeast and incorporate with a little of the flour. Cover and leave to rise for 15 minutes. • Add the salt, spices and remaining liquid to the flour and knead together with the starter dough, until the dough leaves the bowl clean. • Cover and leave to rise, until it has doubled in bulk – this should take about 1 hour. • Butter the baking sheet. • Knead the dough again, then cut into 12 equal-sized pieces and shape into rolls. • Lay them on the baking sheet and brush with lukewarm water. To decorate, sprinkle with the cracked wheat, cover and leave to prove for 15 minutes. • Bake the rolls for 25 minutes in a preheated 220°C/425°F/Gas Mark 7 oven until golden-brown.

Caraway Rolls
illustrated centre

Quantities for 12 rolls:

350g/11oz wholewheat flour

150g/5½oz wholemeal rye flour

42g/1½oz fresh yeast or
21g/¾oz dry yeast

1 tsp sugar

250ml/9 fl oz-375ml/14 fl oz
lukewarm water

2 tsps salt

½ tsp ground caraway seeds

FOR THE DECORATION:

3 tbsps caraway seeds

Greaseproof paper for the baking
sheet

Preparation time: 30 minutes
Rising time: 1½ hours
Baking time: 25 minutes
Nutritional value:
Analysis per roll, approx:
• 545kJ/130kcal
• 5g protein
• 1g fat
• 26g carbohydrate

Mix the flours and make a well in the centre. Crumble in the fresh yeast, stir in the sugar and a little water and flour, cover and leave for 15 minutes. If using dry yeast, blend the yeast with the sugar and water and then pour onto the flour. • Add the salt and ground caraway seeds to the flour, gradually stir in the remaining water and knead it all together with the starter dough, until the dough leaves the bowl clean. • Cover and leave to rise until it has doubled in volume – this should take about 1 hour. • Line the baking sheet with greaseproof paper. • Knead the dough again, cut into 12 equal-sized pieces and shape into balls. Lay the rolls on the baking sheet, make a shallow cross on the surface, brush them with lukewarm water and sprinkle on the caraway seeds. • Cover and leave to rise for 15 minutes. • Bake the rolls in a preheated 220°C/425°F/Gas Mark 7 oven for 25 minutes until golden-brown.

Salty Soft Pretzels

Making your own crispy pretzels is very easy

Quantities for 10 pretzels:

21g/³/₄oz fresh yeast or 10g/¹/₄oz dry yeast
1 tbsp sugar
250ml/9 fl oz lukewarm water
500g/1lb 2oz strong plain white flour
1 tsp salt
15g/¹/₂oz bicarbonate of soda
2 tbsps coarse salt
Butter for the baking sheet

Preparation time: 30 minutes
Rising time: 1¹/₄ hours
Baking time: 30 minutes
Nutritional value:
Analysis per pretzel, approx:
• 795kJ/190kcal
• 6g protein
• 2g fat
• 37g carbohydrate

Dissolve the crumbled fresh yeast or dry yeast with the sugar in a little lukewarm water, cover and leave to froth for 15 minutes at room temperature. • Stir the yeast mixture into the flour, the remaining lukewarm water and salt. Knead the dough thoroughly, cover and leave to rise in a warm place for 1 hour. • Knead the dough thoroughly again and divide into 10 equal-sized pieces. From each piece make a 50cm/20in roll, the middle of which should be as thick as your thumb, with two ends about the thickness of a pencil. Shape into pretzels, pressing the ends up onto the thicker centre part. • Butter the baking sheet. • Dissolve the bicarbonate of soda in 1litre/1³/₄ pints of water and bring to the boil. Take great care with the salt solution; contact with aluminium and skin should be avoided as it is corrosive. • Dip 2 pretzels at a time for ¹/₂ a minute in the boiling salt solution, turning them frequently. Then allow them to dry briefly, lay them on the baking sheet and sprinkle on the coarse salt. • Bake the pretzels on the centre shelf of a preheated 225℃/430°F/Gas Mark 7 oven for 30 minutes until golden-brown. • The pretzels are best eaten warm from the oven.

Buckwheat Crispbread

These crispbreads will keep fresh for at least a week in an airtight metal container

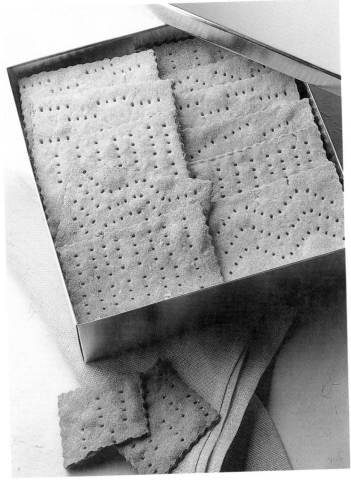

Luxury Rusks

These delicious rusks are a teatime favourite

Buckwheat Crispbread

Quantities for 25 crispbreads:

200g/7oz buckwheat flour and 200g/7oz rye flour
2¼ tsps baking powder
1 tsp ground caraway seeds
1 tsp sea salt
100g/4oz butter
250g/8oz low fat curd cheese
100ml/3 fl oz milk
Butter for the baking sheet

Preparation time: 40 minutes
Rising time: 45 minutes
Baking time: 20-25 minutes
Nutritional value:
Analysis per crispbread, approx:
- 375kJ/90kcal
- 3g protein
- 4g fat
- 11g carbohydrate

Combine the flours in a bowl. Add the baking powder, caraway seeds and salt. • Cut the butter into cubes and add to the mixture, followed by the curd cheese. Stir all the ingredients together and gradually add the milk. Knead the dough thoroughly, cover and leave to rise for 45 minutes. • Butter the baking sheet. • On a lightly floured work surface, roll out the dough to a thickness of 3mm/⅛in. Using a sharp knife or a pastry wheel, cut into 6x10cm/2½x4in strips. • Lay these on the baking sheet and prick with a fork into regular patterns. • Put the crispbreads into a cold oven on the centre shelf, turn the temperature to 200°C/400°F/Gas Mark 6 and bake for 20 to 25 minutes, until hard and brittle. • Spray them with a little cold water and leave to cool on a wire rack.

Luxury Rusks

Quantities for a 30cm/12in baking tin:

6 eggs
½ lemon
8 tbsps maple syrup
½ tsp ground cinnamon
Pinch salt
300g/10oz wholewheat flour
Butter for the baking tin

Preparation time: 40 minutes
Rising time: 12 hours
Baking time: 45 minutes
Baking toast slices: 8 minutes
Nutritional value:
Analysis per slice, if divided into 26 slices, approx:
- 375kJ/90kcal
- 4g protein
- 4g fat
- 10g carbohydrate

Separate the eggs. • Squeeze the juice from the lemon and finely grate the rind. • Beat the egg yolks with the lemon juice, lemon rind, maple syrup and cinnamon until foaming. • Butter the baking tin. • Whisk the egg whites with the salt until they form stiff peaks. • Add the flour to the egg yolk mixture and fold in the egg whites. • Pour the dough into the baking tin and bake on the bottom shelf of a preheated 200°C/400°F/Gas Mark 6 oven for 45 minutes. • Once it has cooled a little, turn out onto a wire rack and leave to stand for 12 hours. • Cut into 26 slices. Bake on the top shelf of a preheated 150°C/300°F/Gas Mark 2 oven for about 4 minutes each side until golden.

Our Tip: As an alternative to cinnamon, use 1 tsp each ground aniseed and vanilla sugar. Different flavours of syrup can also be used. For a nuttier consistency, incorporate 200g/7oz flour and 150g/5½oz finely chopped walnuts into the egg yolk mixture.

Jumbles

The sesame seeds can be mixed into the rolls or sprinkled on top before baking, as in the picture

Quantities for 12 rolls:

300g/10oz strong plain white flour
100g/4oz wheatmeal flour
70g/2¹/₂oz sesame seeds
1 tsp sea salt
21g/³/₄oz fresh yeast or 10g/¹/₄oz dry yeast
2 tsps runny honey
250ml/8 fl oz lukewarm milk
Butter for the baking sheet

Preparation time: 40 minutes
Rising time: 1 hour
Baking time: 15-20 minutes
Nutritional value:
Analysis per roll, approx:
- 630kJ/150kcal
- 6g protein
- 4g fat
- 23g carbohydrate

Pour the flours into a bowl. • Toast half the sesame seeds in a dry pan to draw out the flavour. • Mix the flour with the toasted sesame seeds and salt, make a well in the centre and crumble the fresh yeast into it. Add the honey and wait for 2 minutes, until the yeast has dissolved. If using dry yeast, blend the yeast with the honey and then pour this into the flour. • Stir the milk and a little flour into the yeast mixture, cover and leave to rise at room temperature for 15 minutes. • Knead the starter dough thoroughly with the remaining flour until all the liquid has been absorbed. • Cover and leave to rise for a further 25 minutes. • Butter the baking sheet. • Knead the dough again, adding a little water or flour if necessary. • Divide the dough into 12 equal-sized pieces and shape into balls. Sprinkle the remaining sesame seeds on a work surface and roll out the balls on top into 25cm/10in long sausages. Shape these into rings, place them on the baking sheet, gently press them flat, cover and leave to prove for 20 minutes, during which time the rings should increase in volume by one-third. • Bake the rings on the centre shelf of a preheated 200°C/400°F/Gas Mark 6 oven for 15 to 20 minutes until golden-brown. Remove from the oven, spray with cold water and leave to cool on a wire rack.

Brioches

In France Brioches are enjoyed fresh from the oven for breakfast and in between meals

Quantities for 20 individual brioche tins 8cm/3in in diameter:

750g/1lb 11oz unbleached, strong plain white flour

42g/1½oz fresh yeast or 21g/¾oz dry yeast

50g/2oz icing sugar

125ml/4 fl oz lukewarm milk

200g/7oz butter

5 eggs

1 tsp salt

FOR THE GLAZE:

2 egg yolks

Butter for the tins

Preparation time: 1 hour
Rising time: 1¾ hours
Baking time: 15-20 minutes
Nutritional value:
Analysis per brioche, approx:
• 1210kJ/290kcal
• 9g protein
• 15g fat
• 30g carbohydrate

Sift the flour into a bowl, make a well in the centre and crumble in the fresh yeast. Stir half the icing sugar and a little milk and flour into the yeast, cover and leave to rise for 15 minutes at room temperature. If using dry yeast, blend the yeast with the sugar and milk and then add to the flour. • Melt the butter and leave to cool. • Stir the eggs into the remaining icing sugar and milk, add the salt and butter, pour the mixture onto the edge of the flour and knead all the ingredients thoroughly with the starter dough. • Cover and leave the dough to rise for 1 hour; it should double in volume. • Grease the tins with butter. • Knead the dough again, shape into a roll and cut into 20 pieces. • Mould each piece into one large and one small ball. Put the larger balls in the tins, make a dip on top of each brioche and press the smaller ball into it. • Beat the egg yolks with 1 tbsp water, brush on the brioches, cover and leave to rise for 30 minutes. • Brush the brioches again with the remaining egg yolk and bake on the centre shelf of a preheated 220°C/425°F/Gas Mark 7 oven for 15 to 20 minutes until golden-brown.

Croissants

The classic French croissant is even more delicious when home-baked

Quantities for 15 croissants:

500g/1lb 2oz unbleached, strong plain white flour

$^1/_2$ tsp salt

30g/1oz fresh yeast or 15g/$^1/_2$oz dry yeast

1 tbsp sugar

Just under 250ml/9 fl oz lukewarm milk

300g/10oz butter

1 egg

FOR THE GLAZE:

1 egg yolk

1 tbsp single cream

Butter for the baking sheet

Preparation time: 1$^1/_2$ hours
Rising time: 4 hours
Baking time: 20-25 minutes
Nutritional value:
Analysis per croissant, approx:
• 1380kJ/330kcal
• 7g protein
• 23g fat
• 26g carbohydrate

Sift the flour into a bowl with the salt, make a well in the centre, crumble in the fresh yeast and stir together with the sugar, milk and a little flour. If using dry yeast blend the yeast with the sugar and milk and then add to the flour. Dust the dough with flour, cover and leave in a warm place to rise, until the surface of the flour shows fine cracks – this should take about 20 minutes. • Melt a quarter of the butter and leave to cool. • On a lightly floured work surface, dust the remaining hard butter with flour, roll out to a 15x15cm/6x6in square and place on baking paper in the refrigerator. • Pour the melted butter and egg onto the edge of the flour and mix with the remaining flour and starter dough. Knead the dough for about 20 minutes and knock it back until it is light and elastic. • Cover and leave to rise at room temperature for 45 minutes. • Knead the dough again and, on a floured

work surface, roll out to a 20x35cm/8x14in rectangle. Place the chilled butter square on top, folding the dough over it, and refrigerate for 15 minutes. • Now roll out the dough to a 30x40cm/12x16in rectangle, fold the dough into 3, and return to the refrigerator for another 30 minutes. • Repeat this process three more times, rolling out the rectangle and giving it a quarter turn each time, and leaving it to rest in the refrigerator between rollings. • Finally, roll the dough out to 25x80cm/10x32in strips, make a mark with a sharp knife at 10cm/4in intervals and cut triangles with sides 25cm/10in long. On the 10cm/4in short side make a cut 3cm/1in deep in the centre so that the croissant can be shaped more easily. Roll up the triangles towards the central point and shape into crescents. • Butter the baking sheet , lay the croissants on it a reasonable distance apart, cover and leave to

prove until they have almost doubled in bulk. This will take about 45 minutes. • Beat the egg yolk with the cream, brush the croissants with the mixture and bake them on the centre shelf of a preheated 220°C/425°F/Gas Mark 7 oven for 20 to 25 minutes or until golden-brown. • Enjoy the croissants at their best, still warm from the oven and spread with chilled butter and marmalade.

Our Tip: Croissants are extremely versatile. They taste equally delicious with a sweet nutty filling and a savoury stuffing of minced meat, mushrooms and herbs.

Fresh Breakfast Rolls

These are best served straight from the oven

Milk Rolls with Poppy Seeds
illustrated left

Quantities for 15 rolls:

250g/8oz strong plain flour	
250g/8oz wheatmeal flour	
42g/1¹/₂oz fresh yeast or	
21g/³/₄oz dry yeast	
1 tbsp maple syrup	
250ml/9 fl oz lukewarm milk	
40g/1¹/₂ oz butter	
1 tsp salt	

FOR THE DECORATION AND GLAZE:

2 tbsps maple or golden syrup
3 tbsps black poppy seeds
Butter for the baking sheet

Preparation time: 40 minutes
Rising time: 1³/₄ hours
Baking time: 15-20 minutes
Nutritional value:
Analysis per roll, approx:
• 670kJ/160kcal
• 5g protein
• 4g fat
• 25g carbohydrate

Sift the strong plain white flour into a bowl and combine with the wheatmeal flour. Crumble the yeast into a well in the centre and pour the syrup into it. If using dry yeast, blend with the syrup before pouring over the flour. Stir a little milk and flour into the yeast, cover and leave to rise at room temperature for 15 minutes. • Melt the butter in the remaining milk. • Mix the starter dough into the flour, gradually add the milk and salt, and knead together until the dough is elastic and leaves the bowl clean. • Cover and leave to rise until it has doubled in bulk – this will take about 1 hour. • Butter the baking sheet. • Knead the dough again thoroughly, cut into 15 equal-sized pieces and shape into balls. Flatten the balls slightly and arrange them on the baking sheet. Brush with the syrup and sprinkle on the poppy seeds. • Cover and leave to rise for 30 minutes. • Bake the rolls in a preheated 200°C/400°F/Gas Mark 6 oven for 15 to 20 minutes until golden.

Curd Cheese Rolls
illustrated right

Quantities for 16 rolls:

300g/10oz wholewheat flour
2 tsps caraway seeds
2¹/₄tsps baking powder
1 tsp sea salt
150g/5¹/₂oz soft butter
250g/8oz low fat soft cheese
Butter for the baking sheet

Preparation time: 30 minutes
Rising time: 20 minutes
Baking time: 20 minutes
Nutritional value:
Analysis per roll, approx:
• 585kJ/140kcal
• 4g protein
• 8g fat
• 12g carbohydrate

Mix the wholewheat flour with the caraway seeds, baking powder and salt. • Cut the butter into small pieces and add to the flour with the curd cheese. Mix together and knead thoroughly. • Cover and leave to stand for 20 minutes. • Butter the baking sheet. • Divide the dough into 4 equal-sized pieces and on a floured work surface. Shape each piece into 4 equal-sized balls. Place the rolls on the baking sheet, pressing them down firmly until they are about 1cm/¹/₂in thick and bake on the centre shelf of a preheated 200°C/400°F/Gas Mark 6 oven for about 20 minutes until golden-brown. • Remove the rolls from the oven, spray all over with cold water and leave to cool on a wire rack.

Potato Rolls

This is a traditional Central European recipe

Quantities for 15 rolls:

400g/14oz wholewheat flour
42g/1½oz fresh yeast or 21g/¾oz dry yeast
1 tsp sugar
125ml/4 fl oz each of lukewarm milk and lukewarm water
2 medium onions
1½ tbsps butter
100g/4oz smoked ham
125g/5oz cooked potatoes
8 fresh sage leaves
2 tbsps oil • 1 tsp salt
Pinch of black pepper
Greaseproof paper for the baking sheet

Preparation time: 50 minutes
Rising time: 1¾ hours
Baking time: 25-30 minutes
Nutritional value:
Analysis per roll, approx:
• 545 kJ/130kcal
• 4g protein
• 5g fat
• 20g carbohydrate

Sift the flour into a bowl, make a well in the centre, crumble in the fresh yeast and sprinkle with the sugar. • Mix the milk with the water and stir a little of it into the yeast with a little flour. If using dry yeast, blend the yeast with the milk and water before adding to the flour. Cover and leave to rise at room temperature for 15 minutes. • Peel and finely chop the onions, and fry until transparent in ½ tbsp butter. • Cut the smoked ham into small cubes. Mash the potatoes. Chop the sage leaves. • Knead the starter dough with the rest of the flour and the remaining liquid. Add the onions, ham, potatoes, sage, oil, salt and pepper, cover and leave to rise until it has doubled in bulk – this will take about 1 hour. • Line the baking sheet with greaseproof paper. • Knead the dough again, cut into 15 equal-sized pieces and shape into round rolls. • Cover and leave to rise for 30 minutes. • Cut a cross in the top of each roll. Melt the rest of the butter and brush it over the rolls; bake on the centre shelf of a preheated 200°C/400°F/Gas Mark 6 oven for 25 to 30 minutes.

Dairy Crescents

You can replace the honey in this recipe with the same amount of raw cane sugar

Quantities for 16 crescents:

450g/1lb wholewheat flour

50g/2oz soya flour

42g/1½oz fresh yeast or
21g/¾oz dry yeast

1 tbsp runny honey

250ml/9 fl oz lukewarm milk

1 tsp sea salt

50g/2oz softened butter

FOR THE GLAZE:

4-5 tbsps milk

Butter for the baking sheet

Preparation time: 40 minutes
Rising time: 1 hour
Baking time: 20-25 minutes
Nutritional value:
Analysis per crescent, approx:
- 585kJ/140kcal
- 5g protein
- 5g fat
- 19g carbohydrate

Combine the wheat and soya flours. • Make a well in the centre, crumble the fresh yeast into it and pour on the honey. If using dry yeast, blend the yeast with the honey and then pour onto the flour. Mix the milk with the yeast and a little flour, cover and leave to rise at room temperature for 15 minutes. • Add the salt and butter to the edge of the flour and mix together with the starter dough. Knead the dough thoroughly, cover and leave to rise for 30 minutes. • Butter the baking sheet. • Knead the dough again, adding more water or wholewheat flour if necessary. • Divide the dough into 2 pieces and roll out to 30cm/12in diameter circles. Cut each circle into 8 equal-sized triangles, brush with milk and roll up from the wide side to the point. Mould into crescents, put on the baking sheet, cover and leave to rise for 20 minutes. • Bake the crescents in a preheated 200°C/400°F/Gas Mark 6 oven for 20 to 25 minutes until golden-brown, then spray with cold water and leave to cool on a wire rack.

Sweet Wheatgerm Rolls

For a really crispy finish, prepare these rolls on a surface sprinkled with coarse brown sugar crystals

Quantities for 24 rolls:
800g/1lb 12oz wholewheat flour
60g/2oz soya flour
100g/4oz wheatgerm
84g/3oz fresh yeast or 42g/1½oz dry yeast
4 tbsps Demerara sugar
400ml/14 fl oz lukewarm milk
½ tsp sea salt
100ml/4 fl oz cream
100g/4oz raisins
FOR THE GLAZE:
Milk
Butter for the baking sheet

Preparation time: 1½ hours
Rising time: 2 hours
Baking time: 15-20 minutes
Nutritional value:
Analysis per roll, approx:
• 710kJ/170kcal
• 7g protein
• 4g fat
• 28g carbohydrate

Combine the wholewheat and the soya flour with the wheatgerm. • Make a well in the centre of the flours, crumble the fresh yeast into it, sprinkle with the brown sugar and wait 3 to 4 minutes, until the yeast has dissolved. • Mix the milk with the yeast and a little flour, cover and leave to rise at room temperature for 30 minutes. If using dry yeast, blend the yeast with the milk before adding the flour. • Add the salt and cream to the starter dough, blend and knead thoroughly. • Cover and leave for a further hour. • Wash the raisins in hot water and leave to dry. • Butter the baking sheet. • Knead the dough again, adding the raisins and more milk or flour as required. • Divide the dough into 6 equal-sized pieces and divide each of these into 4 further equal-sized pieces. • Roll 4 of the pieces into 30cm/12in long fingers with tapering ends. Brush the fingers with milk and twist the ends into coils, with one end turning to the right and the other to the left. • Halve the next 4 pieces and roll out to 8 small ovals. Brush them with milk and press 2 ovals together. • Halve the next 4 pieces as well, roll out to 8 pencil-thin strands 40cm/16in in length and brush with milk. Wind 2 strands round one another in a spiral shape like a garland. Press the ends firmly together. • Take 4 more pieces of dough and divide them each into 3 pieces. Mould small balls, brush with milk and stick 3 at a time together. • Roll the next 4 pieces out to 30cm/12in long fingers, brush with milk and mould into large marbles. • Divide each of the last 4 pieces into 3 pieces, roll out to 12 long strands, brush with milk and weave into 4 plaits. • Place on the baking sheet, cover and leave to rise for 30 minutes. • Bake on the centre shelf of a preheated 200°C/400°F/Gas Mark 6 oven for 15 to 20 minutes until golden-brown. Spray with a little cold water and leave to cool on a wire rack.

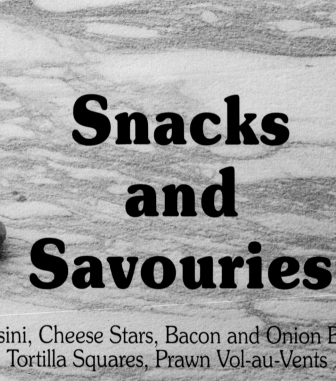

Snacks and Savouries

Grissini, Cheese Stars, Bacon and Onion Biscuits,
Tortilla Squares, Prawn Vol-au-Vents …

Tempting Bread Sticks

Delicious with drinks, and you won't pile on the calories!

Beer Sticks
illustrated in background

Quantities for 32 sticks:

200g/7oz rye flour
200g/7oz wholewheat flour
2 tsps caraway seeds
1 tsp sea salt
2 tbsps sourdough starter mix
1/2 packet dry yeast
1 tbsp raw cane sugar
200g/7oz lukewarm sour cream or thick-set plain yogurt
5 tbsps wine vinegar
4 tbsps sunflower oil
Butter for the baking sheet

Preparation time: 40 minutes
Rising time: 1 hour
Baking time: 30 minutes
Nutritional value:
Analysis per stick, approx:
• 230kJ/55kcal
• 2g protein
• 2g fat
• 8g carbohydrate

Mix the flours in a bowl with the caraway seeds, salt, sourdough starter mix, dry yeast and raw cane sugar. • Make a well in the centre, add the sour cream, vinegar and oil and knead to a smooth dough. Cover and leave to rise at room temperature for 30 minutes. • Divide the dough into 32 equal-sized pieces – it is probably best to weigh them. Shape them into balls and, on a floured work surface, roll out to 20cm/8in long sticks. • Cover and leave to rise for 30 minutes. • Butter a baking sheet. • Arrange the beer sticks on the baking sheet and bake on the centre shelf of a preheated 200°C/400°F/Gas Mark 6 oven for 30 minutes until crispy and slightly brittle. • Spray with a little cold water and leave to cool on a wire rack. • These bread sticks will stay fresh for at least a week in an airtight metal container.

Grissini
illustrated in foreground

Quantities for 60 grissini:

500g/1lb 2oz wheatmeal flour
1 tsp salt
50g/2oz fresh yeast or 25g/1oz dry yeast
Just under 200ml/6 fl oz lukewarm water
1 tsp sugar
6 tbsps olive oil
FOR THE GLAZE:
Milk
Butter or olive oil for the baking sheet

Preparation time: 40 minutes
Rising time: 1 hour
Baking time: 15 minutes
Nutritional value:
Analysis per stick, approx:
• 145 kJ/35kcal
• 1g protein
• 1g fat
• 6g carbohydrate

Mix the flour and salt in a bowl. Make a well in the centre, crumble the fresh yeast into it and mix in the water, sugar and a little flour. If using dry yeast, blend the yeast with the sugar and water and pour onto the flour. Cover and leave to rise at room temperature for 20 minutes. • Knead the starter dough with the remaining flour and olive oil to form a smooth dough which leaves the bowl clean. Cover and leave to rise for 30 minutes. • On a lightly floured work surface roll out the dough to a thickness of 2cm/1in and cut into 10cm/4in long fingers. Roll into sticks about 20 to 25cm/8 to 10in long. • Grease or oil the baking sheet. • Lay the grissini on the baking sheet, cover and leave to rise for 10 minutes; then brush with milk. • Bake on the top shelf of a preheated 220°C/425°F/Gas Mark 7 oven for 15 minutes until golden.

70

Luxury Cheese Assortment

For anyone who enjoys a nibble – and they are delicious with a clear soup

Quantities for 80 biscuits:

250g/8oz wheatmeal flour

1 tsp baking powder

60g/2oz each of Cheddar, Caerphilly and Camembert cheese

200g/7oz chilled butter

1 egg

Pinch each of white pepper, ground nutmeg and sweet paprika

FOR THE GLAZE AND DECORATION:

1 egg yolk

1 tbsp cream

1 tbsp each of chopped peanuts, pistachios, caraway seeds, poppy seeds and sesame seeds

Greaseproof paper for the baking sheet

Preparation time: 1½ hours
Standing time: 1 hour
Baking time: 10 minutes
Nutritional value:
Analysis per biscuit, approx:
- 185kJ/45kcal
- 1g protein
- 4g fat
- 2g carbohydrate

Sift the flour and baking powder on to a work surface.
• Finely grate the Cheddar and Caerphilly and pass the Camembert through a sieve. Sprinkle the cheese over the flour. Cut the butter into knobs and add to the flour. Break the egg into the centre and sprinkle with the spices. Chop the ingredients, then knead to a smooth shortcrust dough. • Cover and refrigerate for 1 hour. • Line the baking sheet with greaseproof paper. • On a lightly floured work surface roll out the dough in 2 portions to a thickness of 5mm/¼in and either cut out 3cm/1in-sized biscuits or, using a pastry wheel, cut small lozenge shapes. • Beat the egg yolk with the cream. • Lay the first batch of biscuits on the baking sheet, brush with the egg yolk and cream and sprinkle the peanuts, pistachios and poppy, caraway and sesame seeds onto alternate biscuits. • Bake on the top shelf of a preheated 220°C/425°F/Gas Mark 7 oven for 10 minutes until golden.

Cashew Biscuits

Lightly spiced with curry

Cheese-and-Herb Rolls

Deliciously tangy – ideal for that between-meals snack

Quantities for 70 biscuits:

150g/5½oz salted cashew nuts

150g/5½oz wheatmeal flour

100g/4oz chilled butter

1 tsp curry powder

Pinch of salt

1 tbsp crème fraîche

2 egg yolks

2-3 tbsps grated Parmesan cheese

For rolling out: clingfilm

Greaseproof paper for the baking sheet

Preparation time: 1½ hours
Standing time: 1 hour
Baking time: 15 minutes
Nutritional value:
Analysis per biscuit, approx:
• 230kJ/55kcal
• 2g protein
• 5g fat
• 2g carbohydrate

Shell the nuts and mix with the flour. Cut the butter into knobs and add to the flour with the curry and salt. Spoon the crème fraîche and 1 egg yolk into the middle. Chop up the ingredients and knead to a smooth, shortcrust pastry. Cover and refrigerate for 1 hour. • Line the baking sheet with greaseproof paper. • Divide the dough into two portions, lay it on clingfilm and roll it out to a thickness of 3mm/⅛in thick. • Cut out 4cm/2in biscuits with a pastry cutter, or use a pastry wheel to cut lozenge shapes. • Beat the remaining egg yolk with 2 tbsps water. • Lay the biscuits on the baking sheet. Brush them with the egg yolk, sprinkle with the Parmesan and bake on the centre shelf of a preheated 200°C/400°F/Gas Mark 6 oven for 15 minutes or until golden.

Quantities for 32 rolls:

100g/4oz strong plain white flour

100g/4oz wheatmeal flour

50g/2oz freshly grated Parmesan cheese

1 tsp baking powder

1 tsp cream of tartar

Pinch each of sea salt and freshly ground white pepper

½ tsp each of dried basil, rosemary and thyme

1 tsp dried parsley

3 eggs

100g/4oz butter

Butter for the baking sheet

Preparation time: 40 minutes
Rising time: 40 minutes
Baking time: 15-20 minutes
Nutritional value:
Analysis per roll, approx:
• 270kJ/65kcal
• 3g protein
• 4g fat
• 4g carbohydrate

Combine the flours and pour them into a bowl. Add the cheese, baking powder, cream of tartar, salt, pepper and crushed herbs and mix thoroughly. • Make a well in the centre, add the eggs and, using a fork, stir in a little of the flour. Cut the butter into knobs and add to the flour. Knead the ingredients together to form a smooth dough. Cover and leave to rise for 40 minutes. • Butter the baking sheet. • Mould the dough into a long roll and divide into 32 equal-sized pieces – it is probably best to weigh them. Shape the pieces of dough into small balls, lay them on the baking sheet and bake on the centre shelf of a preheated 200°C/400°F/Gas Mark 6 oven for 15 to 20 minutes until golden-brown. • These rolls will stay fresh in an airtight metal container for up to 1 week.

Spicy Potato Biscuits

Try frying these instead of baking

Bacon and Onion Biscuits

Delicious savoury shortcrust pastry

Quantities for 40 biscuits:

1kg/2¼lbs floury potatoes

2 garlic cloves

1 bunch of chives

1 tsp salt

Pinch each of ground nutmeg and black pepper

1 tsp dried marjoram

1 egg

100g/4oz wheatmeal flour

100g/4oz freshly grated medium mature Cheddar or Gouda

120g/4½oz chopped sunflower seeds

For the baking sheet and to drizzle: 6 tbsps oil

Cooking time: 30-40 minutes
Preparation time: 40 minutes
Baking time: 25-30 minutes
Nutritional value:
Analysis per biscuit, approx:
• 290kJ/70kcal
• 3g protein
• 4g fat
• 6g carbohydrate

Simmer the potatoes in boiling water for 30 to 40 minutes, peel and, while still hot, press through a sieve. • Finely chop the garlic and chives. • Roughly knead the cooled, mashed potatoes with the garlic, nutmeg, pepper, marjoram, chives, egg, flour and cheese to form a light, workable dough. If necessary, add a little more flour. • Brush the baking sheet generously with oil. • With floured hands, divide the dough into about 40 portions and shape into round, flat biscuits. • Roll both sides of each biscuit in the sunflower seeds and press them in gently. • Lay the potato biscuits on the baking sheet, drizzle a little oil over each one and bake on the centre shelf of a preheated 220°C/425°F/Gas Mark 7 oven for 25 to 30 minutes. • Enjoy the biscuits fresh from the oven.

Quantities for 50 biscuits:

125g/5oz chilled butter

250g/8oz wheatmeal flour

1 egg

Pinch each of salt and ground caraway

1 medium sized onion

100g/4oz streaky bacon

1 tbsp oil

Pinch each of black pepper and ground nutmeg

1 egg yolk

2 tsps caraway seeds

Greaseproof paper for the baking sheet

Preparation time: 1 hour
Standing time: 1 hour
Baking time: 15 minutes
Nutritional value:
Analysis per biscuit, approx:
• 270kJ/65kcal
• 2g protein
• 5g fat
• 4g carbohydrate

Cut the butter into knobs and add to the flour; knead together with the egg, salt and ground caraway seeds. Refrigerate. • Finely chop the onions. Using a sharp knife, remove the rind from the bacon and dice. • Fry the bacon in the oil, add the onions and fry until translucent. • Drain off the fat and leave to cool, then knead the bacon, pepper and nutmeg into the dough. Roll the dough out into a 4cm/2in thick roll, wrap in foil and refrigerate for 1 hour. • Line the baking sheet with greaseproof paper. • Cut the roll of dough into 50 slices. Lay the biscuits on the baking sheet. • Beat the egg yolk with 1 tbsp water, brush over the biscuits. Sprinkle with the caraway seeds. • Bake the biscuits on the centre shelf of a preheated 200°C/400°F/Gas Mark 6 oven for 15 minutes or until golden. • They are at their best served fresh from the oven.

Special Biscuits for Soup

Eat them with soup or use them like croutons

Spicy Savoury Biscuits
illustrated left

Quantities for 30 biscuits:
150g/5^1/$_2$oz wheatmeal flour

20g/^{3}/$_4$oz soya flour

1 tsp baking powder

1 tsp cream of tartar

^{1}/$_2$ tsp each of salt and curry powder

^{1}/$_2$ tsp each of dried basil and parsley

1 egg

100g/4oz butter

1 tbsp golden linseed

Butter for the baking sheet

Preparation time: 40 minutes
Rising time: 1^1/$_2$ hours
Baking time: 15-20 minutes
Nutritional value:
Analysis per biscuit, approx:
• 210kJ/50kcal
• 1g protein
• 4g fat
• 3g carbohydrate

Combine the flours, with the baking powder, cream of tartar, salt, curry and crushed herbs. Pour onto a work surface. • Make a well in the centre, add the egg and mix in a little flour. • Cut the butter into knobs and add to the flour. Knead the ingredients roughly together, cover and leave to rise for 45 minutes. • Shape the dough into 2 rolls of 4cm/2in diameter, turn it in the linseed and press the seeds in gently. • Refrigerate for 45 minutes. • Butter a baking sheet. • Cut the rolls into 5mm/^{1}/$_4$in thick slices. Arrange the biscuits on the baking sheet and bake on the centre shelf of a preheated 200°C/400°F/Gas Mark 6 oven for 15 to 20 minutes until golden-brown.

Salty Savoury Biscuits
illustrated right

Quantities for 25 biscuits:
100g/4oz wheatmeal flour

100g/4oz rye flour

50g/2oz barley flour

50g/2oz rolled oats

1 tsp sea salt

1 tsp baking powder

1 tsp cream of tartar

200ml/7 fl oz single cream

1 egg • 2 tsps runny honey

2 tbsps coarse salt

Butter for the baking sheet

Preparation time: 40 minutes
Rising time: 1^1/$_2$ hours
Baking time: 15-20 minutes
Nutritional value:
Analysis per biscuit, approx:
• 290kJ/70kcal
• 2g protein
• 3g fat
• 8g carbohydrate

Combine the flours and the rolled oats with the salt, baking powder and cream of tartar and tip on to a work surface. • Make a well in the centre, pour in the cream and egg, and mix in a little flour. Work the ingredients to a slightly sticky but elastic dough, then incorporate the honey. • Cover and leave to rise for 45 minutes. • With wet hands shape the dough into 2 rolls of 5cm/2in diameter and leave to dry a little. • Scatter the coarse salt on a work surface, turn the rolls in it and press the salt in gently. • Refrigerate for 45 minutes. • Butter the baking sheet. • Cut the rolls into 5mm/^{1}/$_4$in thick slices, place them on the baking sheet and bake on the centre shelf of a preheated 200°C/400°F/Gas Mark 6 oven for 15 to 20 minutes until golden-brown.

Miniature Salmon Pasties

Favourite snacks in Russia and Poland

Quantities for 25 pasties:
FOR THE DOUGH:
400g/14oz wheatmeal flour
20g/³/₄oz fresh yeast or 10g/¹/₄oz dry yeast
250ml/8 fl oz lukewarm milk
1 tsp sugar • ¹/₂ tsp salt
100g/4oz soft butter
FOR THE FILLING:
1 bunch of pot herbs (leek, carrot, onion, turnip)
1 onion
6 tbsps dry white wine
1 bayleaf
1 tsp each of dried tarragon and white peppercorns
1 tsp salt
300g/10oz salmon steaks
150g/5 ¹/₂oz mushrooms
2 shallots • 1 tbsp butter
2 tbsps finely chopped fresh dill
1 egg
Butter for the baking sheet

Preparation time: 2 hours
Rising time: 30 minutes
Baking time: 30 minutes
Nutritional value:
Analysis per pasty, approx:
• 545kJ/130kcal
• 5g protein
• 6g fat
• 12g carbohydrate

Make a well in the flour, crumble in the yeast, stir in 4 tbsps milk and the sugar. If using dry yeast, blend the yeast with the sugar and milk and pour onto the flour. Cover and leave to rise at room temperature for 15 minutes. • Knead into the starter dough the remaining flour with the salt, 7 tbsps milk and the butter. Cover and leave to rise for 30 minutes. • Bring the pot herbs to the boil with the onions, wine, herbs and salt, and simmer for 10 minutes. • Simmer the salmon in the stock for 10 minutes; leave to cool. • Wipe the mushrooms, chop them and the shallots finely; fry gently in the butter. • Flake the salmon and mix with the dill and mushrooms. • Grease the baking sheet. • Roll the dough out thinly, cut out 25 circles of 9cm/4in diameter. Spoon on the filling and fold up the edges, pressing them together firmly. • Beat the remaining milk with the egg and brush on the pasties; bake in a preheated 200°C/400°F/Gas Mark 6 oven for 30 minutes.

Vegetable Pasties

Pasties can have all sorts of fillings – here is a meatless version

Quantities for 25 pasties:

250g/8oz low fat curd cheese

250g/8oz wheatmeal flour

250g/8oz butter

1 tsp salt

Pinch of ground caraway

250g/8oz each of carrots and courgettes

2 sticks celery

1 onion

1 bunch of chives

2 tbsps olive oil

2 tbsps crème fraîche

3 tbsps grated Parmesan cheese

1 tsp black pepper

1/2 tsp sweet paprika

Pinch of cayenne

1 egg white

2 egg yolks

Greaseproof paper for the baking sheet

Preparation time: 2 hours
Standing time: 30 minutes
Baking time: 25-30 minutes
Nutritional value:
Analysis per pasty, approx:
- 670kJ/160kcal
- 5g protein
- 12g fat
- 9g carbohydrate

Knead the curd cheese with the flour, butter, salt and caraway. Cover and refrigerate for 30 minutes. • Finely grate the scraped carrots and courgettes. • Dice the celery and finely chop the onions and chives. • Fry the onions in the oil until translucent, add the grated vegetables and fry for 5 minutes, then add the celery and fry for a further 3 minutes. • Remove the vegetables from the heat and combine with the chives, crème fraîche, Parmesan and spices. • Line the baking sheet with greaseproof paper. • Roll out the dough very thinly; cut out 25 circles of 8cm/3in diameter and spoon on the vegetable mixture. • Lightly whisk the egg white and brush the edges with it to keep them together. Prick each pasty once with a fork. • Beat the egg yolks. Brush over the pasties. Lay them on the baking sheet and bake on the centre shelf of a preheated 180°C/350°F/Gas Mark 4 oven for 25 to 30 minutes until golden.

Curd Cheese and Butter Snacks

The filling blends perfectly with the delicate pastry

Saffron Turnovers
illustrated left

Quantities for 40 turnovers:
220g/7¹/₂oz wheatmeal flour
220g/7¹/₂oz butter
220g/7¹/₂oz low fat curd cheese
2 pinches of salt
1 sachet ground saffron
1 leek
2 tbsps butter
¹/₂ tsp black pepper
100g/4oz Gorgonzola
2 egg yolks
Greaseproof paper for the baking sheet

Preparation time: 1 hour
Standing time: 45 minutes
Baking time: 15-20 minutes
Nutritional value:
Analysis per turnover, approx:
• 375kJ/90kcal
• 3g protein
• 7g fat
• 4g carbohydrate

Knead the flour with the butter, curd cheese, pinch of salt and saffron. Cover and refrigerate for 45 minutes. • Cut the leek into thin rings and fry in the butter for 5 minutes. Season, leave to cool and combine with the Gorgonzola and 1 egg yolk. • Line the baking sheet with greaseproof paper. • Roll out the dough to a thickness of 5mm/¹/₄in; cut out 40 circles of 7cm/3in diameter and spoon on the filling. Fold up the edges, pressing firmly, and prick each surface once with a fork. • Beat the remaining egg yolk with 1 tbsp water. Brush the crescents with this, place them on the baking sheet and bake on the centre shelf of a preheated 200°C/400°F/Gas Mark 6 oven for 15 to 20 minutes until golden; if possible, serve straight from the oven.

Mini Empanadas
illustrated right

Quantities for 40 empanadas:
250g/8oz wheatmeal flour
250g/8oz each of butter and low fat curd cheese
Pinch of salt • 1 onion
2 preserved chillies
100g/4oz mushrooms
1¹/₂ tbsps raisins
1 hard-boiled egg
2 tbsps oil
250g/8oz minced beef
1¹/₂ tbsps tomato purée
¹/₂ tsp each of salt, black pepper and dried thyme
Pinch of cayenne
2 eggs • 2 tbsps milk
Greaseproof paper for the baking sheet

Preparation time: 1¹/₂ hours
Standing time: 45 minutes
Baking time: 25-30 minutes
Nutritional value:
Analysis per empanada, approx:
• 460kJ/110kcal
• 4g protein
• 8g fat
• 5g carbohydrate

Knead the flour with the butter, curd cheese and salt. Cover and leave in a cool place for 45 minutes. • Finely chop the onions and chillies. Wipe the mushrooms and chop finely. Wash the raisins in hot water. Dice the egg. • Fry the onions in the oil until translucent, add the mince and fry. Add the prepared vegetables, raisins, egg, tomato purée and spices, and cook for 10 minutes. • Line the baking sheet with greaseproof paper. • Separate the eggs. • Roll out the dough extremely thinly, cut out 40 7cm/3in squares. Spoon on the filling, brush the edges with the egg white, fold the squares up into triangles and press the edges firmly. • Beat the egg yolks with the milk and brush on the empanadas; bake in a preheated 200°C/400°F/Gas Mark 6 oven for 25 to 30 minutes.

Olive Pinwheels

Absolutely delicious – especially if served fresh from the oven

Quantities for 24 pinwheels:

21g/³/₄oz fresh yeast or
10g/¹/₄oz dry yeast
Pinch of sugar
125ml/4 fl oz lukewarm water
300g/10oz wheatmeal flour
1 tsp salt
3 eggs
6 tbsps olive oil
100g/4oz almonds
150g/5¹/₂ oz black olives
1 bunch of fresh basil
1 garlic clove
200g/7oz low fat curd cheese
Greaseproof paper for the baking sheet

Preparation time: 1 hour
Rising time: 1³/₄ hours
Baking time: 25-30 minutes
Nutritional value:
Analysis per pinwheel, approx:
• 585kJ/140kcal
• 6g protein
• 8g fat
• 10g carbohydrate

Dissolve the crumbled fresh yeast or dry yeast in the water with the sugar, cover and leave to froth at room temperature for 15 minutes. • Knead the flour, salt, 1 egg and oil into the yeast mixture, until it is no longer sticky. Dust the dough with flour, cover and leave to rise for 1 hour, until it has doubled in bulk. • Cover the almonds with boiling water and remove their skins. • Stone the olives and chop finely with the almonds. • Chop the basil and garlic finely. • Combine the curd cheese with the almond and olive mixture, 1 egg and the herbs. • Line the baking sheet with greaseproof paper. • Roll out the dough to a 40x40cm/16x16in square; spoon on the curd cheese mixture, leaving a strip of 2cm/1in at one side clear. • Roll the dough up firmly and, using a sharp, floured knife, cut into 24 pieces. Lay the pinwheels on the baking sheet and press them down gently. • Beat the remaining egg and brush onto the pinwheels; cover and leave to rise for 30 minutes. • Bake in a preheated 200°C/400°F/Gas Mark 6 oven for 25 to 30 minutes.

Piquant Piped Biscuits

Many other shapes can be made with this piped dough

Phyllo Triangles

These triangles are filled with millet and tender vegetables

Quantities for 60 biscuits:
250g/8oz wheatmeal flour
150g/5¹/₂ oz freshly grated Parmesan cheese
50g/2oz sunflower seeds
175g/6oz soft butter
2 eggs
1 egg yolk
Pinch of sugar
¹/₂ tsp salt
1 tbsp kirsch
Greaseproof paper for the baking sheet

Preparation time: 30 minutes
Standing time: 15 minutes
Baking time: 15 minutes
Nutritional value:
Analysis per biscuit, approx:
• 250kJ/60kcal
• 2g protein
• 4g fat
• 3g carbohydrate

Combine the flour with 100g/4oz of the Parmesan. •

Grind the sunflower seeds; knead with the butter, eggs, egg yolk, sugar, salt, kirsch and the flour and Parmesan mixture to an elastic dough. It should not be too stiff, or it will be difficult to pipe; if necessary, add a little more kirsch. • Line the baking sheet with greaseproof paper. • Put small amounts of dough into the piping bag, fitted with a star-shaped nozzle; pipe the mixture into rings, crescents, sticks and other shapes about 4cm/2in in size onto the baking sheet. • Sprinkle with the remaining Parmesan cheese and stand each sheet in a cool place for 15 minutes before baking. • Bake on the centre shelf of a preheated 180°C/350°F/Gas Mark 4 oven for about 15 minutes or until golden.

Quantities for 20 triangles:
300g/10oz frozen phyllo dough
3 spring onions
200g/7oz mushrooms
1 tbsp lemon juice
1 tbsp oil
1 tsp chopped fresh thyme
4 tomatoes
150g/5¹/₂ oz cooked millet
50g/2oz freshly grated Parmesan cheese
¹/₂ tsp salt
Pinch of white pepper
1 egg yolk

Preparation time: 45 minutes
Baking time: 20 minutes
Nutritional value:
Analysis per triangle, approx:
• 500kJ/120kcal
• 4g protein
• 7g fat
• 11g carbohydrate

Defrost the phyllo dough. • Slice the spring onions, including the green part, into thin rings. Wipe and slice the mushrooms, sprinkle with the lemon juice and fry in the oil over a high heat, stirring constantly, until the liquid has evaporated. • Briefly fry the onion rings and thyme; remove the pan from the heat. • Dice the tomatoes. • Combine the millet with the mushrooms, tomatoes and cheese; season with salt and pepper. • Arrange the phyllo dough sheets one on top of the other on a lightly floured work surface. • Cut the dough into 20 large, equal-sized squares. Spoon on the filling, brushing the edges with water, fold up the squares and press the edges firmly together. • Run the baking sheet under the cold tap. Lay the triangles on the sheet and brush them with the egg yolk. Bake in a preheated 230°C/450°F/Gas Mark 8 oven for 20 minutes until golden.

Pastry Canapés

Their dainty shape makes these canapés particularly appealing

Yeasty Whirls
illustrated left

Quantities for 25 whirls:

21g/³/₄oz fresh yeast or
10g/¹/₄oz dry yeast

125ml/4 fl oz lukewarm milk

Pinch of sugar

250g/8oz wheatmeal flour

Pinch of salt

1 egg yolk • 1 tbsp butter

150g/5¹/₂oz smoked sausage

4 sticks celery

1 tbsp oil

1 tbsp chopped walnuts

Pinch of black pepper

Butter for the baking sheet

Preparation time: 1¹/₄ hours
Rising time: 1 hour
Baking time: 20 minutes
Nutritional value:
Analysis per whirl, approx:
• 375kJ/90kcal
• 3g protein
• 6g fat
• 8g carbohydrate

Dissolve the crumbled fresh yeast or dry yeast in the milk and sugar. Cover and leave to froth at room temperature until it has dissolved. • Combine the flour in a bowl with the salt, add the egg yolk, remaining milk and the butter and knead together with the yeast mixture, until the dough leaves the bowl clean. • Cover and leave to rise at room temperature for 1 hour. • Skin and dice the sausage. Finely chop the celery. • Heat the oil and fry the sausage; add the celery and fry briefly. Dry on absorbent paper, then add the walnuts and season with pepper. • Butter the baking sheet. • Roll out the dough to form a 25x35cm/10x14in rectangle and brush on the filling, leaving a 1cm/¹/₂in wide strip all the way round. Roll the dough up from the short end and cut into 25 pieces. • Lay the coils on the baking sheet and bake on the centre shelf of a preheated 200°C/400°F/Gas Mark 6 oven for 20 minutes or until golden-brown.

Poppy seed Pretzels
illustrated right

Quantities for 30 pretzels:

250g/8oz wheatmeal flour

125g/5oz chilled butter

1 egg yolk

1 tbsp crème fraîche

¹/₂ tsp each of salt, sweet paprika and freshly ground black pepper

3 tbsps black poppy seeds

2 egg yolks

Butter for the baking sheet

Preparation time: 1 hour
Standing time: 40 minutes
Baking time: 15-20 minutes
Nutritional value:
Analysis per pretzel, approx:
• 420kJ/100kcal
• 3g protein
• 7g fat
• 6g carbohydrate

Put the flour in a bowl, cut the butter into knobs and add; then mix in the egg yolk, crème fraîche, salt, paprika and pepper, and knead to form an elastic dough. • Shape into a roll of around 3cm/1in in diameter, cover and refrigerate for 40 minutes. • Butter the baking sheet. • Cut the dough roll into 30 pieces; on a lightly floured work surface shape into 17cm/7in long cylinders and shape these into mini-pretzels. • Pour the poppy seeds onto a plate. Beat the egg yolks with a little water. Brush the egg yolks on the pretzels and turn them gently in the poppy seeds. Arrange them on the baking sheet and bake in a preheated 180°C/350°F/Gas Mark 4 oven for 15 to 20 minutes.

Cheese Parcels

Instead of feta, try using the mint-flavoured cheese from Cyprus, known as Halloumi

Quantities for 25 parcels:

250g/8oz wheatmeal flour
1 egg
1-2 tbsps lukewarm water
3 tbsps olive oil
Pinch of salt
1 tsp balsamic vinegar
50g/2oz stoned black olives
250g/8oz feta cheese
1/2 tsp each of salt and freshly ground black pepper
1 tsp dried oregano
2 tbsps chopped pistachio nuts
1 egg yolk
100g/4oz melted butter
1 bunch of chives
Butter for the baking sheet

Preparation time: 1 hour
Standing time: 30 minutes
Baking time: 30 minutes
Nutritional value:
Analysis per parcel, approx:
• 545kJ/130kcal
• 4g protein
• 9g fat
• 8g carbohydrate

Put the flour in a bowl. Beat the egg with the water, oil, salt and vinegar, combine with the flour and knead until it is no longer sticky. Cover and refrigerate for 30 minutes. • Chop the olives finely, crumble on the feta cheese and add the salt, pepper, crushed oregano, pistachios and egg yolk. • Butter the baking sheet. • On a floured work surface roll the dough out thinly, to an 80x120cm/32x47in rectangle. If necessary, you can stretch it further, using the backs of your hands. • Brush the melted butter on the rolled out dough. Cut out 25 circles of 8cm/3in diameter and spoon on the filling. Bring the edges up over the filling, pressing together to form little parcels. • Lay the parcels on the baking sheet and bake on the centre shelf of a preheated 180°C/350°F/Gas Mark 4 oven for 30 minutes, basting frequently with the remaining butter. • Wind 1 chive round each cooled parcel as decoration.

Ham Crescents

Use the best Italian raw ham, or substitute smoked beef

Quantities for 16 crescents:

500g/1lb 2oz strong plain flour

21g/³/₄oz fresh yeast or
10g/¹/₄oz dry yeast

1 tsp sugar

250ml/9 fl oz lukewarm water

1 tsp salt

2 onions

250g/8oz lean, raw ham

2 tbsps butter

2 tbsps chopped fresh parsley

Pinch of white pepper

1 egg

1 egg yolk

3 tbsps milk

Greaseproof paper for the baking sheet

Preparation time: 1 hour
Rising time: 1 hour
Baking time: 15 minutes
Nutritional value:
Analysis per crescent approx:
• 710kJ/170kcal
• 6g protein
• 5g fat
• 24g carbohydrate

Make a well in the flour, crumble in the yeast and stir in the sugar, a little flour and a little lukewarm water. If using dry yeast, blend with the sugar and water and pour onto the flour. Cover and leave to froth at room temperature for 15 minutes. • Add salt and remaining water to the flour and knead to form a smooth dough. Cover and leave to rise for 30 minutes. • Finely chop onions and ham. • Heat the butter and fry the onions until translucent; add ham and parsley and fry briefly. Remove mixture from the heat, season with the pepper and combine with the beaten egg. • Line the baking sheet with greaseproof paper. • Roll the dough to form 2 circles 36cm/14in in diameter. Cut each circle into 8 triangles; spoon on the filling and shape into crescents by rolling up the triangles. Arrange crescents on the baking sheet and leave to stand for 15 minutes. • Beat the yolk with the milk, brush on the crescents and bake in a preheated 220°C/425°F/Gas Mark 7 oven for about 15 minutes.

Ham and Cheese Diamonds

These are delicious served with wine, and complement vegetable soups well

Quantities for 60 diamonds:

150g/5¹/₂oz wheatmeal flour

150g/5¹/₂oz wholemeal flour

21g/²/₃oz fresh yeast or
10g/¹/₄oz dry yeast

1 tsp sugar

125ml/4 fl oz lukewarm water

2 tbsps butter • ¹/₄ tsp salt

1 onion

1 tsp butter

150g/5¹/₂oz each of cooked and raw ham, fat removed

3 eggs

125ml/4 fl oz single cream

100g/4oz double cream

100g/4oz grated Cheddar cheese

Butter for the baking sheet

Preparation time: 45 minutes
Rising time: 1¹/₂ hours
Baking time: 40 minutes
Nutritional value:
Analysis per diamond, approx:
• 290kJ/70kcal
• 3g protein
• 5g fat
• 4g carbohydrate

Mix the flours in a bowl, make a well in the centre, crumble in the yeast and stir in the sugar and half the water. If using dry yeast, blend the yeast with the sugar and water and pour onto the flour. Cover and leave to froth at room temperature for 15 minutes. Cover and leave to rise for 15 minutes. • Melt the butter in the remaining water and knead with the salt, starter dough and remaining flour. Cover and leave to rise for 45 minutes. • Chop the onions and fry in the butter until translucent. • Cut the ham into strips. • Beat the eggs with the single and double cream; combine with the ham and onion. • Butter half the baking sheet. • Roll out the dough to the size of half the sheet, place it on the sheet and leave to rise for 30 minutes. • Spoon the ham mixture over the dough; sprinkle on the cheese. • Bake on the centre shelf of a preheated 210°C/410°F/Gas Mark 6 oven for 40 minutes; cut into 60 diamonds.

Mouthwatering Savouries

These are at their best served hot

Bacon Bakes
illustrated left

Quantities for 50 rolls:

400g/14oz fat bacon
Pinch of dried sage
500g/12oz wheatmeal flour
15g/¹/₂oz butter
1 tsp salt
Just under 300ml/11 fl oz cold water
1 egg yolk
Butter and flour for the baking sheet

Preparation time: 45 minutes
Standing time: 2 hours
Baking time: 12 minutes
Nutritional value:
Analysis per roll, approx:
- 95kJ/95kcal
- 2g protein
- 6g fat
- 7g carbohydrate

Remove the rind from the bacon. Cut the bacon into cubes, mince with the mugwort and cook on a low heat. Strain through a sieve and allow the fat to harden. • Work the flour and butter, salt and water to a stiff dough. Roll it out to a thickness of about 1.5cm/²/₃in, in a 32x42cm/12x16in rectangle. • Spoon the bacon fat onto half of the rolled out dough and fold the other half on top. Leave to stand in a cool place for 30 minutes. • Roll the dough out again to a thickness of 1.5cm/²/₃in, fold together again and leave to stand in a cool place for a further 30 minutes. • Repeat the whole process again twice at half-hourly intervals. • Butter the baking sheet and dust it with flour. • Roll the dough out again to a thickness of 1.5cm/²/₃in and cut out rounds 5cm/2in in diameter. Place them on the baking sheet, brush with the beaten egg yolk and bake in a preheated 200°C/400°F/Gas Mark 6 oven for 12 minutes.

Herb and Cheese Diamonds
illustrated right

Quantities for 1 baking sheet:

200g/7oz rye flour
200g/7oz wheatmeal flour
1 tbsp yeast
2 tbsps sourdough starter mix
About 250ml/9 fl oz lukewarm water
1 tsp honey
1 tsp salt
2 bunches fresh dill
300g/10oz freshly grated Parmesan cheese
3 eggs
300g/10oz crème fraîche
Pinch of white pepper
Lard for the baking sheet

Preparation time: 30 minutes
Rising time: 1³/₄ hours
Baking time: 25 minutes
Nutritional value:
Analysis per slice, if divided into 30 slices, approx:
- 630kJ/150kcal
- 7g protein
- 9g fat
- 12g carbohydrate

Mix the flours with the yeast, sourdough extract, water, honey and salt and knead into a stiff, workable dough. Cover and leave to rise in a warm place, until it has doubled in volume – this will take about 1 hour. • Grease the baking sheet with lard. • Roll the dough out on the baking sheet and prick all over with a cocktail stick. • Pull the leaves off the dill stalks and chop finely. • Combine the Parmesan cheese with the eggs, crème fraîche, pepper and dill and spread over the dough. Cover and leave to rise for 40 minutes. • Bake on the centre shelf of a preheated 200°C/400°F/Gas Mark 6 oven for about 25 minutes.

Prawn Packets

A tempting surprise for special occasions

Quantities for 16 packets:

FOR THE DOUGH:

100g/4oz butter

150ml/5 fl oz water

350g/11oz wheatmeal flour

$^1/_2$ tsp salt

1 tsp raw cane sugar

FOR THE FILLING:

16 peeled, cooked prawns

Juice of $^1/_2$ a lemon

Pinch of freshly ground white pepper

1 garlic clove

2 shallots

300g/10oz spinach

$^1/_2$ tsp salt

4 tbsps crème fraîche

1 egg yolk

Greaseproof paper for the baking sheet

Preparation time: 1 hour
Standing time: 10 minutes
Baking time: 40-50 minutes
Nutritional value:
Analysis per packet, approx:
• 710kJ/170kcal
• 6g protein
• 9g fat
• 17g carbohydrate

Bring the butter and water to the boil. • Mix the flour with the salt and sugar in a bowl, add the boiling water and stir to form a dough. Wrap the dough in clingfilm and leave to stand for 20 minutes. Place a bowl over the dough as it needs to be still warm when worked again. • Drizzle the lemon juice onto the prawns and season with pepper. • Finely chop the garlic clove and shallots. • Wash the spinach and cook without extra water until it wilts. Leave to drain. • Combine the garlic, shallots and salt with the spinach. • Brush the prawns with the crème fraîche and wrap in the spinach leaves. • Line the baking sheet with greaseproof paper. • Divide the dough into 16 portions. Roll out each portion, wrap the prawns in dough and press the edges together. • Lay the envelopes on the baking sheet. Beat the egg yolk, brush on the envelopes and bake on the centre shelf of a preheated 200°C/400°F/Gas Mark 6 oven for 40 to 50 minutes.

Wholemeal Recipes for the Store Cupboard

Just right when you're a little peckish

Buckwheat Fingers
illustrated left

Quantities for 48 fingers:

100g/4oz strong plain white flour
50g/2oz buckwheat flour
50g/2oz fine cornmeal
1 tsp baking powder
1 tsp cream of tartar
Pinch of sea salt
1/2 tsp black pepper
2 eggs
100g/4oz butter
100g/4oz feta cheese
Butter for the baking sheet

Preparation time: 40 minutes
Rising time: 45 minutes
Baking time: 15-20 minutes
Nutritional value:
Analysis per finger, approx:
- 710kJ/170kcal
- 1g protein
- 3g fat
- 3g carbohydrate

Combine the flours with the cornmeal, baking powder, cream of tartar, salt and spices. Pour onto a work surface, make a well in the centre, break in the eggs and stir in a little flour. • Cut the butter into knobs and add to the flour. • Mash the cheese to a creamy paste and knead with the butter and other ingredients to form an elastic dough. • Cover and leave to rise for 45 minutes. • Butter the baking sheet. • Divide the dough into 4 pieces. Form 12 equal-sized balls out of each piece of dough and roll out to 10cm/4in long fingers. Lay the fingers on the baking sheet and bake on the centre shelf of a preheated 200°C/400°F/Gas Mark 6 oven for 15 to 20 minutes until golden-brown.

Spicy Cheese Patties
illustrated right

Quantities for 40 patties:

100g/4oz wheatmeal flour
100g/4oz rye flour
125g/5oz freshly grated Cheddar, Emmental or Gouda cheese
1 tsp baking powder
1 tsp cream of tartar
Pinch of sea salt
1 tsp caraway seeds
1/2 tsp each of fennel seeds and coriander
1 egg
150g/51/2oz butter
100g/4oz sour cream
2 tbsps caraway seeds
Butter for the baking sheet

Preparation time: 30 minutes
Rising time: 1 3/4 hours
Baking time: 15 minutes
Nutritional value:
Analysis per patty approx:
- 250kJ/60kcal
- 2g protein
- 5g fat
- 3g carbohydrate

Combine the flours with the cheese, baking powder, cream of tartar salt and spices. Pour onto a work surface and make a well in the centre. Break in the egg and stir in a little flour. • Cut the butter into knobs and add to the flour. Knead the ingredients together to form an elastic dough; work in the sour cream. Cover and leave to rise for 45 minutes. • Shape the dough into 2 rolls of 5cm/2in diameter. Turn the rolls in the caraway seeds, pressing the seeds in gently. Cover and refrigerate for 30 minutes. • Butter the baking sheet. • Cut the dough rolls into 5mm/1/4in thick slices, lay them on the baking sheet and bake on the centre shelf of a preheated 200°C/400°F/Gas Mark 6 oven for 15 minutes.

Deep-Fried Delights

These snacks are at their best served fresh from the fryer

Deep-Fried Cheese Rings
illustrated left

Quantities for 70 rings:

250ml/9 fl oz water	
100g/4oz butter	
1/2 tsp salt	
Pinch of nutmeg	
175g/6oz wheatmeal flour	
4 eggs	
80g/3oz freshly grated Parmesan cheese	
1 tbsp sesame seeds	
For frying: 1l/1 3/4 pints oil	

Preparation time: 25 minutes
Cooking time per portion:
4-6 minutes
Nutritional value:
Analysis per ring, approx:
• 230kJ/55kcal
• 1g protein
• 4g fat
• 2g carbohydrate

Bring the water, butter, salt and nutmeg to the boil. Add the flour and stir until the dough leaves the pan clean, forming a ball. Put the dough in a bowl, leave to cool slightly and gradually stir in the eggs, cheese and sesame seeds. • Heat the oil in a deep fat fryer to 175°C/350°F. • Place the dough in a piping bag with a small star nozzle and pipe small rings onto lightly greased baking parchment. Slip the rings into the hot oil in small quantities, fry for 2 to 3 minutes on each side, remove from the oil with a slotted spoon and leave to drain on absorbent paper.

Stuffed Fried Triangles
illustrated right

Quantities for 35 triangles:

FOR THE DOUGH:	
42g/1 1/2oz fresh yeast or	
21g/3/4oz dry yeast	
250ml/9 fl oz lukewarm milk	
Pinch of sugar	
1 tsp salt	
500g/12oz wheatmeal flour	
1 egg	
50g/2oz lard	
FOR THE FILLING:	
150g/5 1/2oz Mozzarella cheese	
100g/4oz cooked ham	
3 sprigs of lemon balm	
100g/4oz low fat curd cheese	
2 tbsps grated Parmesan cheese	
1/2 tsp black pepper	
1/4 tsp sweet paprika	
1 tsp lemon juice	
1 egg	
1 egg white	
FOR FRYING: 1l/1 3/4 pints oil	

Preparation time: 1 hour
Rising time: 30 minutes
Cooking time per portion:
4 minutes
Nutritional value:
Analysis per triangle, approx:
• 460kJ/110kcal
• 5g protein
• 6g fat
• 11g carbohydrate

Crumble the yeast into a bowl, dissolve in the milk, add all the other dough ingredients and knead thoroughly. If using dry yeast, blend the yeast with the sugar and milk and pour onto the flour and other yeast ingredients. Cover and leave to froth at room temperature for 15 minutes. Cover and leave to rise at room temperature for 30 minutes. • Dice the cheese and ham. Finely chop the lemon balm leaves; combine with the cheese and ham cubes, curd cheese and Parmesan. Season with the spices and lemon juice, and add the egg. • Knead the dough again, roll out to a thickness of 4mm and cut into 35 10cm/4in squares. • Spoon the filling onto the squares. Brush the edges with whisked egg white and fold up into triangles. Press the edges firmly with a fork. • Heat the oil to 175°C/350°F in a deep fat fryer. • Fry the triangles in the hot oil in small quantities for 2 minutes on each side and leave to drain on absorbent paper.

Meat and Vegetable Envelopes

These are particularly easy if frozen puff pastry is used

Quantities for 20 envelopes:

300g/10oz wheatmeal flour
½ tsp salt
2 egg yolks
150g/5½oz butter
150g/5½oz carrots
1 leek
1 shallot
1 garlic clove
1 bunch of fresh parsley
150g/5½oz rindless streaky bacon
½ tsp dried thyme
1 tsp lemon juice
1 tsp green peppercorns
Butter for the baking sheet

Preparation time: 1 hour
Standing time: 30 minutes
Baking time: 20-25 minutes
Nutritional value:
Analysis per envelope, approx:
- 840kJ/200kcal
- 4g protein
- 15g fat
- 12g carbohydrate

Mix the flour in a bowl with the salt and 1 egg yolk. Add the cubed butter and knead to form a smooth dough. Cover and refrigerate for 30 minutes. • Scrape and dice the carrots. Cut the leek into thin rings. Finely chop the shallots, garlic and parsley. • Dice the bacon and fry in a pan until the fat begins to run. Add the shallots and garlic and fry until translucent. • Add the carrots and leek and fry gently for 5 minutes, stirring constantly. • Combine the vegetables with the parsley, crushed thyme, lemon juice, peppercorns and a pinch of salt. • Butter the baking sheet. • Roll out the dough to a thickness of 3mm; cut out 20 squares and spoon on the filling, bringing the edges up round the filling. • Brush the envelopes with the remaining beaten egg yolk, place on the baking sheet and bake on the centre shelf of a preheated 200°C/400°F/Gas Mark 6 oven for 20 to 25 minutes until golden-brown.

Three-Cheese Tartlets

These can be frozen and reheated – and they taste like they've been freshly baked

Quantities for 25 tartlets:

500g/1lb 2oz wheatmeal flour
1 packet dry yeast
Pinch of sugar
1 tsp salt
Just under 250ml/9 fl oz lukewarm milk
125g/5oz Brie
125g/5oz feta cheese
250g/8oz low fat curd cheese
1 tbsp butter
1 egg
1 egg yolk
1 bunch of parsley
Butter for the baking sheet

Preparation time: 1 hour
Rising time: 1 hour
Baking time: 20-25 minutes
Nutritional value:
Analysis per tart, approx:
- 840kJ/200kcal
- 7g protein
- 5g fat
- 15g carbohydrate

Knead the flour, yeast, sugar, salt and milk to form an elastic dough. Dust with flour, cover and leave to rise in a warm place, until it has doubled in volume – this should take about 45 minutes. • Purée the Brie and feta cheese, stir in the curd cheese, butter and egg. • Butter the baking sheet. • Knead the dough again; on a floured work surface roll out to a thickness of 4mm and cut out 25 circles of 10cm/4in diameter. Spoon on the filling and bring the edges up 1cm/$^{1}/_{2}$in wide over the filling. • Lay the tarts on the baking sheet and brush the edges with the beaten egg yolk. • Cover and leave to rise for 15 minutes. • Bake the tarts on the centre shelf of a preheated 200°C/400°F/Gas Mark 6 oven for 20 to 25 minutes until golden. • Serve the tartlets warm, garnished with the chopped parsley.

Spicy Tartlets

Made with frozen puff dough or shortcrust dough

Tomato Tartlets
illustrated left

Quantities for 8 12cm/5in tartlet tins:

300g/10oz frozen puff dough
10 small tomatoes
150g/5¹/₂oz Mozzarella cheese
1 tbsp freshly grated medium mature Cheddar or Gouda cheese
3 eggs
4 tbsps crème fraîche
¹/₂ tsp each of salt, freshly ground black pepper and dried oregano
2 bunches fresh basil

Preparation time: 30 minutes
Baking time: about 15 minutes
Nutritional value:
Analysis per tartlet, approx:
- 1215kJ/290kcal
- 12g protein
- 20g fat
- 15g carbohydrate

Defrost the puff pastry. • Pour boiling water over 8 tomatoes, skin them and cut into eighths. Dice the Mozzarella. Beat the grated cheese with the eggs and crème fraîche; season with the salt, pepper and oregano. Wash and dry the basil, put aside 8 attractive leaves, coarsely chop the others and add to the egg mixture. • Run the tins under the cold tap. • Roll the pastry out as thinly as possible; line the tins with the pastry, pressing it up the sides. • Arrange the tomato eighths in a star shape in the tins, sprinkle on the Mozzarella and pour on the egg mixture. • Arrange the tins on a baking sheet and bake them on the baking sheet on the bottom shelf of a preheated 220°C/425°F/Gas Mark 7 oven for 5 minutes. Reduce the temperature to 200°C/ 400°F/Gas Mark 6 and transfer to the centre shelf. Bake for a further 8 to 10 minutes until golden-brown. • Garnish with the basil leaves and tomato slices; serve hot or cold.

Leek Tartlets
illustrated right

Quantities for 8 8cm/3in tins:

200g/7oz wheatmeal flour
80g/3oz chilled butter
1 egg yolk
Pinch of salt
3 bunches of chives
250g/8oz full fat curd cheese
1 egg
1 egg yolk
Pinch each of salt and freshly grated nutmeg
¹/₂ tsp ground white pepper
Butter for the tins

Preparation time: 40 minutes
Standing time: 30 minutes
Baking time: 20 minutes
Nutritional value:
Analysis per tartlet, approx:
- 1300kJ/310kcal
- 12g protein
- 22g fat
- 19g carbohydrate

Knead the flour, cubed butter, egg yolk, salt and 2 to 3 tbsps of cold water together to form a smooth dough. Cover and refrigerate for 30 minutes. • Finely chop the chives. Stir the curd cheese into the egg and egg yolk, season with salt, nutmeg and pepper, and add the chives. • Grease the tins with butter. • Roll out the dough as thinly as possible and line the tins with it. Prick the dough base all over with a fork and bake on the bottom shelf of a preheated 200°C/400°F/Gas Mark 6 oven for 5 minutes. Now add the chive mixture to the tartlets and bake for a further 15 minutes on the centre shelf. • Serve warm as a starter, or otherwise cold.

Stuffed Puff Pastry Snacks

These can be made in a trice using frozen puff dough

Roast Veal Crescents
illustrated left

Quantities for 26 crescents:

300g/10oz frozen puff dough	
1 onion	
1/2 tbsp butter	
1 gherkin	
1/2 bunch of parsley	
40g/1 1/2oz Gorgonzola cheese	
200g/7oz roast veal	
Pinch each of salt, freshly ground nutmeg and white pepper	
1/2 tsp grated lemon rind	
2 egg yolks	
2 tbsps milk	

Preparation time: 1 1/4 hours
Baking time: 20 minutes
Nutritional value:
Analysis per crescent, approx:
• 460kJ/110kcal
• 3g protein
• 8g fat
• 4g carbohydrate

Defrost the puff dough. • Chop the onions; fry in the butter until translucent. Dice the gherkin. Chop the parsley; combine with the onion, gherkin, crumbled Gorgonzola and roast veal. Season the mixture with the salt, nutmeg, pepper and lemon rind. • Roll out the puff dough as thinly as possible. Cut out 13 10cm/4in squares and halve them diagonally. • Spoon the filling onto the triangles, roll them up and shape into crescents. Run the baking sheet under the cold tap, then lay the crescents on it. • Beat the egg yolks with the milk, brush onto the crescents and bake on the centre shelf of a preheated 200°C/400°F/Gas Mark 6 oven for 20 minutes until golden. Serve hot or cold.

Spinach Triangles
illustrated right

Quantities for 22 triangles:

300g/10oz frozen puff dough	
300g/10oz spinach	
1 small onion	
2 tbsps olive oil	
2 garlic cloves	
150g/5 1/2oz feta cheese	
1/2 tsp each of salt and freshly ground black pepper	
1 tsp dried oregano	
2 egg yolks	

Preparation time: 1 hour
Baking time: 20 minutes
Nutritional value:
Analysis per triangle, approx:
• 460kJ/110kcal
• 4g protein
• 9g fat
• 5g carbohydrate

Defrost the puff dough. • Wash the spinach thoroughly and cut down the stalks. Chop the onions. Heat the oil in a pan and fry the onions until translucent. Crush the garlic cloves; add to the pan with the spinach. Fry gently for 5 minutes and press through a sieve. • Crumble the feta cheese and add to the salt, pepper and oregano; combine with the spinach mixture. • Roll out the puff dough as thinly as possible. Cut out 22 8cm/3in squares. Spoon on the filling and fold up the sides to form triangles. Press the edges firmly with a fork. • Run the baking sheet under the cold tap; place the triangles on it. Beat the egg yolks with 1 tbsp water and brush onto the triangles. Bake on the centre shelf of a preheated 200°C/400°F/Gas Mark 6 oven for 20 minutes until golden. Serve warm.

Our tip: These triangles can also be made from phyllo dough.

Tofu Puffs

This is a good opportunity to try tofu if you've never used it before

Quantities for 12 puffs:
300g/10oz frozen phyllo dough
350g/11oz tofu
2 spring onions
100g/4oz canned bamboo shoots
1 tsp salt
1/4 tsp freshly ground white pepper
2 tbsps dark soy sauce
1 egg yolk
2 tbsps milk
FOR THE SAUCE:
2 shallots
2 garlic cloves
2 tbsps oil
4 tbsps tomato ketchup
3 tbsps dark soy sauce
1 tsp sugar

Preparation time: 45 minutes
Baking time: 25 minutes
Nutritional value:
Analysis per puff, approx:
- 710kJ/170kcal
- 5g protein
- 11g fat
- 12g carbohydrate

Defrost the phyllo dough. • Dice the tofu. Chop the spring onions. Drain the bamboo shoots, cut into small cubes and combine with the tofu and onions. Season with the salt, pepper and soy sauce. • Cut the phyllo dough into 12 15x12cm/6x5in rectangles. Spoon on the filling, press down gently and brush the edges with water. Fold the sides together and press down firmly on the edges. • Beat the egg yolk with the milk and brush onto the puffs. Run the baking sheet under the cold tap; place the puffs on it and bake on the centre shelf of a preheated 220°C/425°F/Gas Mark 7 oven for 25 minutes until golden. • Chop the shallots and garlic; fry in the oil until translucent. Stir in the ketchup, soy sauce, 4 tbsps water and the sugar. Bring the sauce to the boil and simmer for 5 minutes. • Leave the tofu puffs to cool slightly; serve with the warm sauce.

Party Mini Pizzas

Ideal finger food for parties

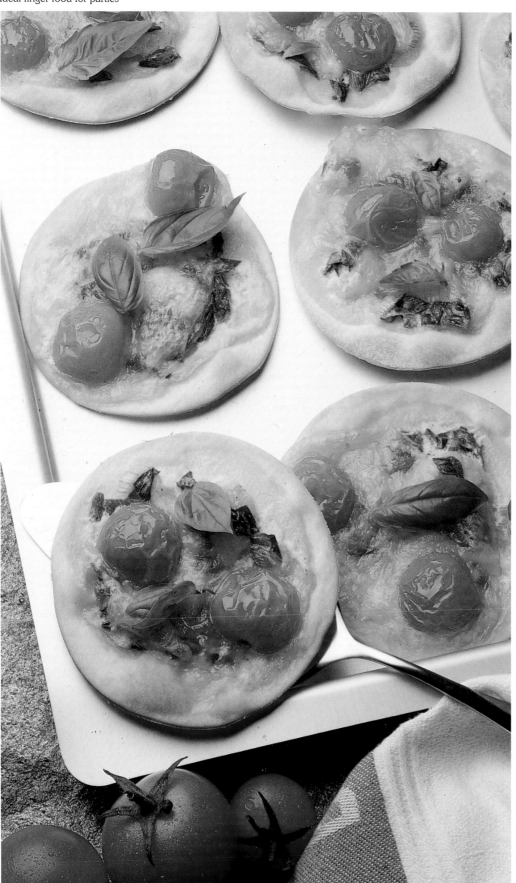

Quantities for 20 pizzas:

250g/8oz low fat curd cheese
1 tsp salt
4 tbsps olive oil
2 eggs
500g/12oz wheatmeal flour
4 small spring onions
1 garlic clove
1 tbsp butter
1 tbsp crème fraîche
50g/2oz peeled, cooked prawns
1 tbsp freshly grated medium mature Cheddar or Gouda cheese
Pinch each of salt and freshly ground black pepper
80g/3oz Mozzarella cheese
20 cherry tomatoes
½ bunch of basil
Greaseproof paper for the baking sheet

Preparation time: 1 hour
Baking time: 10 minutes
Nutritional value:
Analysis per pizza, approx:
- 630kJ/150kcal
- 7g protein
- 5g fat
- 19g carbohydrate

Stir the salt, oil and eggs into the curd cheese; add the flour in spoonfuls, beating well to incorporate after each addition. Roll the dough into a ball and refrigerate. • Finely chop the spring onions. Crush the garlic. • Fry the onions gently in the butter for 5 minutes, add the garlic, stir in the crème fraîche and leave to cool. Combine the prawns with the Cheddar or Gouda, salt, pepper and onions. • Cut the Mozzarella into 10 slices. Halve the cherry tomatoes. Pinch off the basil leaves. • Line the baking sheet with greaseproof paper. • Roll out the pastry as thinly as possible. Cut out 20 10cm/4in circles and place on the baking sheet. • Spoon the onion mixture onto 10 slices and cover the 10 others with 1 slice of Mozzarella and a basil leaf. Season. • Garnish each mini-pizza with 2 tomato halves; bake on the bottom shelf of a preheated 200°C/400°F/Gas Mark 6 oven for 10 minutes. • Serve fresh from the oven.

Miniature Favourites

Perfect for those special occasions

Savoury Choux Puffs
illustrated left

Quantities for 60 puffs:

250ml/9 fl oz water

150g/5oz butter

Pinch of salt

Pinch of celery salt

175g/6oz wheatmeal flour

3 eggs

400g/14oz calves liver

3 tbsps dry sherry

150g/5½oz soft butter

½ tsp each of salt and freshly ground white pepper

3 tbsps chopped chives

Greaseproof paper for the baking sheet

Preparation time: 1 hour
Baking time: 20 minutes
Assembly: 20 minutes
Nutritional value:
Analysis per puff, approx:
• 250kJ/60kcal
• 2g protein
• 4g fat
• 2g carbohydrate

Bring the water to the boil with 100g/4oz of the butter, the salt and celery salt. Add the flour and beat until the dough forms a ball. Transfer to a bowl, leave to cool and beat the eggs into it one by one. • Line the baking sheet with greaseproof paper. • Put the dough in a piping bag with a small star nozzle and pipe 60 balls (about the size of a cherry) on the baking sheet. • Bake on the centre shelf of a preheated 220°C/ 425°F/Gas Mark 7 oven for 20 minutes or until golden; leave to cool. • Cut the liver into thin strips and brown in the rest of the butter. Cut into cubes and blend in a liquidizer. Combine with the sherry, butter, salt, pepper and chives, and chill until set. • Cut the puffs in half horizontally. Spread the liver paste on the bottom half and pop the lid on top.

Mini-Brioches
illustrated right

Quantities for 20 4cm/2in tins:

250g/8oz wheatmeal flour

15g/½oz fresh yeast or
8g/¼ oz dry yeast

1 tsp sugar

6 tbsps warm milk

100g/4oz sliced salami

3 tbsps chopped chives

100g/4oz butter

2 eggs

Pinch of salt

Grated rind of 1 lemon

1 egg yolk • 2 tsps cream

Butter for the tins

Preparation time: 1 hour
Rising time: 1 hour
Baking time: 15-20 minutes
Nutritional value:
Analysis per brioche, approx:
• 585kJ/140kcal
• 5g protein
• 10g fat
• 9g carbohydrate

Pour the flour into a bowl and make a well in the centre. Crumble in the fresh yeast, mix with the sugar, milk and a little of the flour. If using dry yeast, blend it with the sugar and milk and pour onto the flour. Cover and leave to rise for 20 minutes. • Remove the skin from the salami, chop into very small cubes and combine with the chives. Melt the butter and knead with the eggs, salt, lemon rind, salami, remaining flour and starter dough, until it becomes smooth and elastic. Cover and leave to rise for 40 minutes. • Grease the tins with butter. • Shape the dough into a roll, divide into 20 pieces and shape each into 2 balls, one the size of a walnut and the other cherry-sized. • Place the larger balls in the tins, make an indentation in the centre and set the smaller balls on top. • Beat the egg yolk with the cream. Brush onto the brioches and bake in a preheated 220°C/425°F/Gas Mark 7 oven for 15 to 20 minutes.

Pizzas, Flans and Quiches

Delicious pastry concoctions filled with vegetables,
meat and cheese – just right for a casual evening
entertaining friends

Favourite Pizzas

You can let your imagination run riot with pizza toppings

Four Season Pizza
illustrated left

Quantities for 2 pizzas:
21g/³/₄oz fresh yeast or 10g/¹/₄oz dry yeast

¹/₂ tsp sugar

125ml/4 fl oz lukewarm water

300g/10oz wheatmeal flour

6 tbsps olive oil • ¹/₂ tsp salt

400g/14oz tomatoes

200g/7oz mushrooms

150g/5¹/₂oz lean, cooked ham

50g/2oz salami • 2 red chillies

4 anchovy fillets

300g/10oz can artichoke hearts

Pinch pepper, salt and rosemary

100g/4 oz grated Parmesan

Olive oil for the baking sheet

Preparation time: 1 hour
Rising time: 1 hour
Baking time: 30 minutes
Nutritional value:
Analysis per pizza, approx:
• 6720kJ/1600kcal
• 86g protein
• 79g fat
• 130g carbohydrate

Mix the fresh yeast with the sugar and water, and allow to rise for 15 minutes. If using dry yeast, blend with the sugar and water and pour onto the flour. • Knead the flour, 4 tbsps oil and the salt into the yeast mixture; cover and allow to rise for 45 minutes. • Peel and slice the tomatoes; slice the mushrooms; cut ham and salami into strips; snip the anchovies and the chillies, and cut the artichoke hearts into slices. • Lightly oil two baking sheets. • Shape the dough into two circles with slightly raised edges, mark each one into four quadrants with a knife, and place on the baking sheets. • Arrange tomatoes, mushrooms, ham with the chillies and the artichokes with the salami on the quarters of the pizza; sprinkle with seasoning, rosemary, anchovies and Parmesan cheese; drizzle oil over the topping. Bake on the centre shelf of a preheated 220°C/425°F/Gas Mark 7 oven for 30 minutes.

Napoletana

Quantities for 2 pizzas:
21g/³/₄oz fresh yeast or 10g/¹/₄oz dry yeast

¹/₂ tsp sugar

125ml/4 fl oz lukewarm water

300g/11oz wheatmeal flour

5 tbsps olive oil • ¹/₂ tsp salt

400g/14oz large tomatoes

1 onion • 1 garlic clove

150g/5¹/₂oz Mozzarella cheese

4 sprigs of basil • 20 black olives

¹/₂ tsp each of dried oregano, black pepper and salt

Olive oil for the baking sheet

Preparation time: 40 minutes
Rising time: 1 hour
Baking time: 30 minutes
Nutritional value:
Analysis per pizza, approx:
• 4620kJ/1100kcal
• 36g protein
• 52g fat
• 120g carbohydrate

Mix the yeast with the sugar and water, and leave to rise for 15 minutes. If using dry yeast, blend the yeast with the sugar and water and pour onto the flour. • Knead the flour, 3 tbsps of the oil and the salt into the yeast mixture, cover and leave to rise for 45 minutes. • Slice the tomatoes, and cut the onions into rings. Crush the garlic. Chop the mozzarella into cubes. Pinch the leaves off the sprigs of basil. • Lightly oil two baking sheets. • Knead the dough thoroughly and shape it into two circles 20cm/8in in diameter, with slightly raised edges; place on the baking sheets. • Arrange the tomatoes, onions and cheese on the base; sprinkle on the olives, basil, garlic and seasoning, and drizzle oil over each pizza. • Bake on the centre shelf of a preheated 220°C/430°F/Gas Mark 7 oven for 30 minutes.

Deep Pan Wholewheat Pizza

This pizza is particularly delicious if you use fresh, rather than dried, mixed herbs

Quantities for 1 baking sheet:

250g/8oz tinned chickpeas
300g/11oz wholewheat flour
42g/1¹/₂oz fresh yeast or 21g/³/₄oz dry yeast
1 tsp honey
125ml/4 fl oz lukewarm water
1 tsp sea salt
9 tbsps olive oil
1 bunch of spring onions
1 green pepper
1 red pepper
1 yellow pepper
100g/4oz black olives
200g/7oz crème fraîche
200g/7oz tomato purée
1 tbsp mixed herbs
¹/₂ tsp black pepper
¹/₂ tsp sweet paprika
150g/6oz grated pecorino cheese
Butter for the baking sheet

Preparation time: 1 hour
Baking time: 25 minutes
Nutritional value:
Analysis per piece, when cut into 20 slices, approx:
- 1005kJ/240kcal
- 10g protein
- 15g fat
- 15g carbohydrate

Combine the honey, yeast, half the water and 2 tbsps flour. Cover and allow to rise for 15 minutes. • Knead the salt, 3 tbsps oil, the rest of the flour and the yeast starter together, cover and allow to rise for 25 minutes. • Deseed the peppers, then cut the onions into rings and the peppers into strips. Stone the olives and chop them roughly. • Whisk together the crème fraîche, tomato purée, the rest of the water, the remaining oil and the herbs and spices. • Roll out the dough on a greased baking sheet, cover and leave to rise for 15 minutes. • Drain the chickpeas, and spread them over the dough, together with the onions, peppers and olives, then pour the tomato purée mixture over the pizza and sprinkle it with the cheese. • Bake in a preheated 200°C/400°F/Gas Mark 6 oven for 25 minutes.

Potato and Tomato Pizzas

Vary the spicing to suit your taste

Tomato Pizza
illustrated left

Quantities for 2 pizzas:

300g/10oz wheatmeal flour
1/2 packet dry yeast
1 tsp salt • 8 tbsps olive oil
150ml/5 fl oz lukewarm water
1 1/4kg/2 3/4lbs tomatoes
2 garlic cloves
1 tsp dried oregano
1 tsp dried thyme
Pinch of sugar
1/2 tsp black pepper
2 bunches of spring onions
300g/10oz Mozzarella cheese
75g/3oz grated Parmesan cheese
Butter for the baking sheet

Preparation time: 40 minutes
Rising time: 1 hour
Baking time: 30 minutes
Nutritional value:
Analysis per pizza, approx:
• 6300kJ/1500kcal
• 70g protein
• 70g fat
• 130g carbohydrate

Mix the flour with the yeast, a generous pinch of salt, 4 tbsps oil and the water, and knead together. Cover and leave to rise for 1 hour. • Peel the tomatoes and slice four of them; dice the rest. • Crush the garlic and fry in 1 tbsp of oil until translucent. Add the chopped tomatoes, herbs, 1/2 tsp of salt, sugar and pepper, and simmer until the sauce thickens. • Slice the onions into rings. Cut the Mozzarella into cubes. • Divide the dough in half and roll each half into a circle with a slightly raised edge. Pour the tomato sauce on the pizzas, put the slices of tomato and onion rings on top, and sprinkle on a pinch of salt, the Mozzarella and the Parmesan. Drizzle on the olive oil. Bake the pizzas in a preheated 200°C/400°F/Gas Mark 6 oven for 30 minutes.

Potato Pizza
illustrated right

Quantities for 2 pizzas:

300g/10oz wheatmeal flour
1/2 packet dry yeast
1 tsp salt
5 tbsps olive oil
100ml/3 fl oz lukewarm water
700g/1 1/2lbs new potatoes
200g/7oz mushrooms
2 small leeks
100g/4oz grated Parmesan cheese
125ml/4 fl oz cream
1/2 tsp white pepper
1 tbsp fresh rosemary
Butter for the baking sheet

Preparation time: 45 minutes
Rising time: 1 hour
Baking time: 40 minutes
Nutritional value:
Analysis per pizza, approx:
• 5790kJ/1380kcal
• 52g protein
• 52g fat
• 178g carbohydrate

Mix the flour and half the salt with the yeast. Add 2 tbsps of the oil and the water, and knead together. Cover and leave to rise for 1 hour. • Peel and thinly slice the potatoes, blanch in boiling water for two minutes, rinse in cold water and drain. • Wipe and dice the mushrooms. Finely chop the leeks. • Mix the mushrooms with the leeks and stir in the cheese and cream. Season with salt and pepper. • Chop the rosemary. • Butter two baking sheets. • Divide the dough in half and roll each half into a circle with a slightly raised edge. Pour the mushroom mixture over the dough and arrange layers of potatoes on top. Sprinkle with salt and rosemary. Drizzle the olive oil over the topping. • Bake the pizzas on the centre shelf of a preheated 200°C/400°F/Gas Mark 6 oven for 40 minutes.

Focaccia con cece

This Italian flatbread is made with chickpeas

Quantities for 1 baking sheet:
500g/17oz wholewheat flour
42g/1½ oz fresh yeast or 21g/¾oz dry yeast
2 tsps runny honey
375ml/13 fl oz lukewarm water
2 tsps sea salt
250g/8oz canned chickpeas
50g/2oz butter, cut into knobs
Butter for the baking sheet

Preparation time: 45 minutes
Rising time: 50 minutes
Baking time: 30 minutes
Nutritional value:
Analysis per piece, when cut into 16 slices, approx:
- 585kJ/140kcal
- 5g protein
- 4g fat
- 21g carbohydrate

Pour the flour into a bowl. Make a well in the centre, crumble in the fresh yeast, sprinkle with the honey and wait until the yeast has dissolved. If using dry yeast, blend the yeast with the honey and water and pour this over the wheat flour. • Mix the yeast mixture with the water, salt and a little flour. Cover and allow to rise for 15 minutes. • Drain the chick-peas and knead them together with 1 tsp salt, the starter dough and the rest of the flour. Leave the dough to rise for a further 20 minutes. • Butter the baking sheet. • Knead the dough, then roll it out to a 30x30cm/12x12in square. Lay it on the baking sheet, cover and allow to rise until it has increased in volume by one-third. • Sprinkle the remaining salt on the dough. Using a teaspoon handle, make indentations in the dough and put the cubed butter in them. • Bake the flatbread for 25-30 minutes on the centre shelf of a preheated 200°C/400°F/Gas Mark 6 oven until golden-brown. Spray with cold water, leave to cool and cut into 20 slices.

Focaccia with pine-nuts

Eat this Italian flatbread while still hot – spread with butter

Quantities for 8 flatbreads:

400g/14oz wholewheat flour
1 tsp dried rosemary
2 tsps dried basil
Pinch freshly ground black pepper
42g/1½ oz fresh yeast or 21g/¾oz dry yeast
2 tsps runny honey
250ml/9 fl oz lukewarm water
5 garlic cloves
6 tbsps olive oil
1 tsp sea salt
40g/1½oz pine nuts
Butter for the baking sheet

Preparation time: 40 minutes
Rising time: 1 hour
Baking time: 30 minutes
Nutritional value:
Analysis per focaccia, approx:
• 1090kJ/260kcal
• 7g protein
• 10g fat
• 34g carbohydrate

Combine the flour in a bowl with the herbs and pepper. Make a well in the middle, crumble in the fresh yeast, sprinkle on the honey; wait until the yeast has dissolved. If using dry yeast, blend the yeast with the honey and pour onto the wheat grains. • Mix the water and the yeast mixture with a little of the flour, cover, and leave to rise for 15 minutes. • Crush the garlic cloves and fry gently in 5 tbsps of oil until translucent. Cool briefly and knead together with all of the flour, the starter dough and the salt. Cover and leave to rise for 20 minutes. • Knead the dough again, mixing in the pine nuts. • Butter two baking sheets. • Divide the dough into 8 balls, flatten them into 12cm/5in rounds, place on the baking sheets, cover and allow them to rise until they have increased in volume by one-third. • Prick the focaccia with a fork, drizzle on the remaining oil, and bake on the centre shelf of a preheated 200°C/400°F/Gas Mark 6 oven until golden-brown. • Spray cold water on the finished focaccia and leave to cool.

Pizzas with Prawns, Fish and Vegatables

These pizzas offer deeply satisfying toppings – whether you prepare them small for guests or full sized for family meals

Celery Pizza
illustrated left

Quantities for 12 small pizzas:
400g/14oz tomatoes
1 onion • 2 garlic cloves
2 tbsps olive oil
1 generous tsp salt
1 tsp black pepper
1 sprig of basil
250g/8oz low fat curd cheese
2 eggs • 5 tbsps olive oil
500g/1lb 2oz wheatmeal flour
300g/10oz celery
3 spring onions
200g/7oz smoked salmon
2 tbsps butter
5 tbsps grated Parmesan cheese
Oil for the baking sheet

Preparation time: 1 hour
Baking time: 40 minutes
Nutritional value:
Analysis per pizza, approx:
• 1300kJ/310kcal
• 52g protein

• 14g fat
• 34g carbohydrate

Peel and chop the tomatoes. Finely chop the onion and garlic, and fry in the oil until translucent. Add the tomatoes, pinch of salt and ¹/₂ tsp pepper; simmer for 30 minutes. • Chop the basil and stir it into the tomato mixture. • Drain the curd cheese and combine it with the remaining salt, pepper and oil; knead it into the flour. Place the dough in the refrigerator. • Thinly slice the celery and spring onions. Cut the smoked salmon into strips. • Fry the vegetables gently in butter for 2 minutes and add the smoked salmon. • Divide the dough into 12 pieces, press into small, flat rounds and place on 2 greased baking sheets. • Pour the tomato mixture onto the pizzas and spoon the vegetable mix on top. Sprinkle on the grated Parmesan, and bake in a preheated 200°C/400°F/Gas Mark 6 oven for 25 minutes.

Pizza Capricciosa
illustrated right

Quantities for 2 pizzas:
200g/7oz wheatmeal flour
10g/¹/₄oz fresh yeast or 5g/¹/₈oz dry yeast
25ml/4 fl oz lukewarm water
400g/14oz tomatoes
2 tbsps tomato purée
Pinch each of salt and pepper
3 tbsps olive oil
200g/7oz tinned artichoke hearts
100g/4oz Mozzarella cheese
200g/7oz peeled, cooked prawns
¹/₂ tsp dried oregano

Preparation time: 1 hour
Rising time: 1 hour
Baking time: 20-25 minutes
Nutritional value:
Analysis per pizza, approx:
• 2310kJ/550kcal
• 39g protein
• 18g fat
• 53g carbohydrate

Sift the flour into a bowl, scrumble in the fresh yeast, mix in the water and a little of the flour. If using dry yeast, blend the yeast with the sugar and water and pour onto the flour. Cover and leave to rise for 15 minutes. • Peel and chop the tomatoes, mix with the tomato purée, salt and pepper, and cook until the liquid has been absorbed. • Knead together the flour, starter dough, pinch of salt and 1 tbsp of oil; cover and leave to rise for 45 minutes. • Drain artichoke hearts and chop into quarters; cut cheese into cubes. • Grease two baking sheets. • Roll out the dough into two circles with slightly raised edges, and place on the baking sheets. Spread the tomatoes, artichoke hearts, prawns and cheese on the pizzas, and sprinkle on the oregano. Drizzle on the remaining oil. • Bake in a preheated 220°C/425°F/Gas Mark 7 oven for 20 to 25 minutes.

Spicy Flans with an Unusual Flavour

These savoury flans are the perfect dish for a buffet or informal party

Savoury Mango Flan

illustrated left

Quantities for 1 26cm/10in flan:

20g/³/₄ oz fresh yeast or 10g/¹/₄oz dry yeast
Pinch of sugar
150g/5¹/₂oz natural yogurt
2 tbsps clarified butter
250g/8oz wheatmeal flour
¹/₂ tsp salt
1 tbsp tomato purée
3 tbsps mango chutney
1 ripe mango
5 shallots
1 tbsp sesame seeds
Butter for the quiche dish

Preparation: 1 hour
Rising time: 45 minutes
Baking time: 25 minutes
Nutritional value:
Analysis per piece, if divided into 12 slices, approx:
• 545kJ/130kcal
• 3g protein
• 3g fat
• 21g carbohydrate

Dissolve the crumbled fresh yeast or dry yeast with the sugar in 2 tbsps of warm water; leave to froth for 15 minutes. • Warm the yogurt. Melt the clarified butter and mix with the yogurt, yeast mixture, flour and salt; knead thoroughly. • Cover and leave in a warm place until the dough has doubled in volume. • Grease the quiche dish. Roll out the dough into a circle, place in the dish, and brush with the remaining clarified butter. Mix the tomato purée and mango chutney and spread onto the flan base. • Peel the mango and cut it in thin slices radiating out from the stone; arrange in a star pattern on the flan. • Thinly slice the shallots and arrange between the mango slices. Sprinkle on the sesame seeds. • Bake the flan on the bottom shelf of a preheated 180°C/350°F/Gas Mark 4 oven for 25 minutes and serve hot.

Breton Mussel Flan

illustrated left

Quantities for 1 26cm/10in flan:

250g/8oz wheatmeal flour
125g/5oz butter
4 eggs
275g/9oz pickled mussels
2 garlic cloves
2 tbsps chopped fresh parsley
2 tbsps brandy
250ml/¹/₂pt cream
Pinch each of white pepper and cayenne
1 tsp grated lemon rind
Butter for the quiche dish

Preparation time: 40 minutes
Standing time: 30 minutes
Baking time: 45 minutes
Nutritional value:
Analysis per piece, if divided into 12 slices, approx:
• 1215kJ/290kcal
• 9g protein
• 20g fat
• 16g carbohydrate

Make a dough with the flour, butter, 1 egg, 2 tbsps cold water and pinch of salt; knead together, cover in clingfilm and put in a cool place for 30 minutes. • Drain the mussels. • Crush the garlic; place in a bowl. Add the parsley, brandy, cream and remaining eggs, whisk thoroughly and season with a pinch of salt and the herbs. Mix in the mussels. • Roll out the dough, place in the quiche dish and press up the sides. • Bake the flan on the centre shelf of a preheated 200°C/400°F/Gas Mark 6 oven for 45 minutes. If the surface browns too rapidly, cover with aluminium foil.

Stuffed Naan

An unleavened bread with a slightly sweet, fruity flavour

Quantities for 2 naan:
80g/3oz dried apricots
80g/3oz raisins
1 tbsp raw cane sugar
125ml/4 fl oz buttermilk
42g/1½ oz fresh yeast or 21g/¾oz dry yeast
45g/1½oz clarified butter (ghee)
2 eggs
550g/20oz wheatmeal flour
½ tsp salt
1 tsp ground cardamom
150g/5½oz mixed nuts
2 tbsps milk
Butter for the baking sheet

Preparation time: 30 minutes
Soaking time: 12 hours
Rising time: 1 hour
Baking time: 25 minutes
Nutritional value:
Analysis per naan, approx:
• 8400kJ/2000 kcal
• 61g protein
• 77g fat
• 270g carbohydrate

Wash the raisins and dried apricots, cover with warm water and soak for 12 hours. • Gently heat the clarified butter and sugar, dissolve the crumbled fresh yeast or the dry yeast in the mixture and leave for 15 minutes. • Stir 2 tbsps melted clarified butter into the eggs and whisk thoroughly. • Mix flour with the salt, cardamom, eggs and yeast mixture, and knead into a workable dough; if necessary, add some of the water in which the fruit has been soaking. Cover the dough and leave until doubled in volume.• Butter two baking sheets. • Divide the dough into four parts, roll each one into a circle and lay two of the circles on the baking sheets. • Roughly chop the dried fruit and nuts, mix them together and spread them on the pastry bases. Moisten edges of the pastry with water, lay the two remaining pastry circles on top and press the edges together. Combine remaining clarified butter with the milk and brush the top of the pastry with the mixture. • Bake the naan for 15 minutes on the centre shelf of a preheated 220°C/425°F/Gas Mark 7 oven, and then for 10 minutes on the oven floor.

Hearty Traditional Pies

The secret of a great pie is light pastry

Cheese and Pine Nut Pie
illustrated left

Quantities for 1 26cm/10in pie:

300g/10oz frozen puff pastry

8 preserved vine leaves

1 leek

1 garlic clove

200g/7oz feta cheese

3 eggs

200g/7oz low fat curd cheese

100g/4oz full fat soft cheese

1 tbsp capers

1/2 tsp salt

20g/3/4oz pine nuts

Butter for the pie dish

Preparation time: 40 minutes
Baking time: 50 minutes
Nutritional value:
Analysis per piece, if divided into
12 slices, approx:
• 1000kJ/240kcal
• 11g protein
• 17g fat
• 11g carbohydrate

Defrost the frozen puff pastry. • Wash the vine leaves and pat them dry on kitchen paper. Chop the leek. Finely chop the garlic. • Lay the sheets of pastry one on top of the other and roll them out to the shape of the quiche dish. Line the dish with the pastry and arrange the vine leaves on top. • Work the feta cheese through a sieve and mix into a creamy paste with the eggs, curd cheese, soft cheese, capers, salt, garlic and chopped leek. • Spread the mixture onto the vine leaves and sprinkle on the pine nuts. • Bake on the centre shelf of a preheated 200°C/400°F/Gas Mark 6 oven for 50 minutes; serve hot or cold.

Sauerkraut Pie
illustrated right

Quantities for 1 32cm/12in pie:

350g/11oz floury potatoes

100g/4oz butter

200g/7oz buckwheat flour

30g/1oz soya flour

1 tsp sea salt

1 1/4 tsp baking powder

200g/7oz rindless streaky bacon

4 onions

4 tbsps sunflower oil

1kg/2 1/4 oz sauerkraut, rinsed

200g/7 fl oz sour cream

Pinch of black pepper

1 tsp sweet paprika

4 bay leaves • 1 egg yolk

Butter for the quiche dish

Preparation time: 40 minutes
Cooking time: 40 minutes
Baking time: 35-40 minutes
Nutritional value:
Analysis per piece, if divided into
16 slices, approx:
• 1090kJ/260kcal
• 6g protein
• 19g fat
• 17g carbohydrate

Peel the potatoes and boil until soft, then mash with the butter. Mix the buckwheat flour and potatoes and combine with the soya flour, baking powder and salt, and knead together. • Dice the bacon and onions. • Fry bacon in the oil until crispy, put aside half of the bacon and mix the onion in with the rest; fry until golden. • Chop the sauerkraut. • Whisk the sour cream and spices and combine with the onion and bacon mixture, and the sauerkraut. Butter the pie dish, pour in the sauerkraut mixture and add the bay leaves. • Roll out the pastry, cut into strips 4cm/2in wide, and lay these across the sauerkraut in a crisscross pattern. • Beat the egg yolk with a little water and use it to glaze the pastry. Press the remaining cubes of bacon into the glaze. • Bake the pie on the centre shelf of a preheated 200°C/400°F/Gas Mark 6 oven for 35 to 40 minutes.

Hearty Meat and Cheese Pies

These can be served fresh from the oven, or cold with a glass of wine

Roquefort Pie
illustrated left

Quantities for 1 26cm/11in pie:
450g/1lb frozen puff pastry
1 onion
250g/8oz mushrooms
25g/1oz butter
1 garlic clove
2 spring onions
4 tbsps dry white wine
600g/1¹/₂lbs small, floury potatoes
200g/7oz Roquefort or Stilton
¹/₂ tsp each of salt and freshly ground black pepper
1 tsp dried thyme
1 egg yolk

Preparation time: 1 hour
Baking time: 1¹/₄ hours
Nutritional value:
Analysis per piece, if divided into 8 slices, approx:
• 1800kJ/2430kcal
• 12g protein
• 28g fat
• 32g carbohydrate

Defrost the puff pastry. • Chop the onions. • Wipe and slice the mushrooms; fry gently with the onion until the liquid has been absorbed. • Crush the garlic and add to the onion mixture. • Slice the spring onions and add to the onions with the wine; simmer gently for 5 minutes. • Peel and slice the potatoes. • Crumble the Roquefort or Stilton. • Roll out two-thirds of the pastry and line the pie dish with it. Arrange half the potatoes on it and season with a little salt, pepper and thyme. • Then add a layer of mushrooms and sprinkle cheese on top. Continue with these layers, seasoning each one, until all the ingredients have been used up. • Roll out the remaining pastry and lay it on top of the filling, pressing the edges together. • Brush with egg yolk and bake in a preheated 180°C/350°F/Gas Mark 4 oven for 1¹/₄ hours.

Chestnut and Pork Fillet Pie
illustrated right

Quantities for 1 26cm/11in pie:
250g/8oz wheatmeal flour
125g/5oz butter
1 egg
1 tbsp milk
1 tsp salt
300g/10oz pork fillet
400g/14oz small, floury potatoes
300g/10oz can of chestnut purée
4 eggs
1 tsp freshly ground black pepper
3 tbsps chopped chives
Butter for the springform tin

Preparation time: 45 minutes
Standing time: 30 minutes
Baking time: 40 minutes
Nutritional value:
Analysis per piece, if divided into 12 slices, approx:
• 1385kJ/330kcal
• 14g protein
• 17g fat
• 31g carbohydrate

Combine the flour, butter, egg, milk and pinch of salt to form a dough; cover and refrigerate for 30 minutes. • Skin the pork fillet, remove the fat and dice. Peel and slice the potatoes. • Whisk the chestnut purée with the eggs, season with the remaining salt and the pepper, and combine with the chives, potato slices and pork cubes. • Butter the tin. • Roll out two-thirds of the dough and line the tin with it, pressing up the sides. Spread the chestnut filling over the bottom. • Roll out the rest of the dough and lay it on top of the filling, pressing the edges together. • Bake in a preheated 200°C/400°F/Gas Mark 6 oven for 40 minutes.

Orange and Mushroom Quiche

The subtly bitter flavour of the oranges lends this dish an unusual tang

Quantities for 1 26cm/11in quiche dish:

500g/1lb 2oz mushrooms
200g/7oz low fat curd cheese
200g/7oz wheatmeal flour
200g/7oz chilled butter
Pinch each of salt and freshly ground white pepper
1 egg yolk
1 onion
2 tbsps butter
100g/4oz herbed cream cheese
2 eggs
1/2 tsp salt
2 oranges
Butter for the quiche dish

Preparation time: 1 hour
Standing time: 1 hour
Baking time: 30 minutes
Nutritional value:
Analysis per piece, if divided into 12 slices, approx:
• 1300kJ/310kcal
• 10g protein
• 23g fat
• 15g carbohydrate

Wipe the mushrooms, mince and leave to stand uncovered so that they turn brown and really develop their flavour. • Knead the curd cheese together with the flour, knobs of butter, salt and egg yolk. Cover and leave in the bottom of the refrigerator for 1 hour. • Grease the tin with butter. • Roll out the pastry and line the tin with it. • Finely chop the onions and fry in the butter until golden. Work the mushrooms through a fine mesh sieve, add to the onions and fry until the liquid has been absorbed. • Combine the cheese with the eggs, mushroom purée, salt and pepper and spread onto the pastry. • Wash the oranges in warm water and, leaving the rind on, slice very thinly. Arrange them on top of the mushroom filling, bake on the centre shelf of a preheated 200°C/400°F/Gas Mark 6 oven for 30 minutes and serve hot.

Spinach Pie

Delicious served hot with cream of horseradish sauce

Quantities for 1 24cm/9in pie:
400g/14oz flour
¹/₂ tsp salt
250g/8oz butter
1kg/2¹/₄lbs spinach
2 shallots • 1 garlic clove
¹/₄ tsp each of salt and pepper
50g/2oz pine nuts
4 hard boiled eggs
125ml/4 fl oz each of milk and cream
1 egg yolk • 1 tbsp flour
2 tbsps grated Parmesan cheese
2 tbsps olive oil
Butter for the tin

Preparation time: 1 hour
Standing time: 30 minutes
Baking time: 1 hour
Nutritional value:
Analysis per piece, if divided into 8 slices, approx:
- 2895kJ/690kcal
- 20g protein
- 49g fat
- 42g carbohydrate

Knead the flour with the salt, 200g/7oz of the butter and 8 tbsps of ice-cold water. Cover and refrigerate for 30 minutes. • Wash the spinach, blanch for 2 minutes and drain thoroughly. • Chop the shallots and garlic. • Melt the remaining butter and fry the spinach, shallots, garlic, salt and pepper gently for 10 minutes. Add the pine nuts. • Grease the pie dish. • Roll out two-thirds of the dough to a 32cm/13in circle and line the dish with it. Pour in half the spinach. Roll out the remaining pastry. Cut the eggs in half and arrange in a circle on the spinach. Then put the remaining spinach on top. • Whisk the milk with the cream, egg yolk, flour and cheese and pour on. • Lay the pastry lid on top, pressing the edges down firmly, and make a 3cm/1in hole in the centre. • Brush the quiche with oil and bake in a preheated 220°C/425°F/Gas Mark 7 oven for 1 hour.

Bacon and Apple Quiche

A tasty snack with a hint of sweet and sour

Quantities for 1 26cm/11in springform tin:
200g/7oz wheatmeal flour
Pinch each of baking powder and salt
1 egg
50g/2oz ground hazelnuts
100g/4oz butter
2 bunches of spring onions
600g/1¹/₂lbs tart apples
100g/4oz crème fraîche
1 tsp raw cane sugar
120g/4oz rindless streaky bacon in strips
Butter for the tin

Preparation time: 40 minutes
Standing time: 1 hour
Baking time: 45 minutes
Nutritional value:
Analysis per piece, if divided into 12 slices, approx:
- 1300kJ/310kcal
- 5g protein
- 23g fat
- 20g carbohydrate

Knead the flour together with the baking powder, salt, egg, nuts and cubed butter. Shape into a ball, cover and refrigerate for 1 hour. • Cut the spring onions in half and slice into 3cm/1in pieces. • Peel, halve and core the apples; cut into slices. • Butter the tin • Roll the pastry out to a circle and line the tin with it, pressing it up the sides. Bake blind on the centre shelf of a preheated 200°C/400°F/Gas Mark 6 oven for 15 minutes. • Spread the crème fraîche on the pastry base and arrange the apple slices in alternate layers with the onions; sprinkle with the raw cane sugar and bacon. • Bake for 30 minutes.

Mushroom and Vegetable Quiches

Moist, juicy fillings in crispy shortcrust pastry

Savoy Cabbage and Tomato Quiche
illustrated left

Quantities for 1 28cm/11in springform tin:

250g/8oz wholewheat flour

1 tsp salt

4 eggs

125g/5oz soft butter

400g/14oz tomatoes

300g/10oz Savoy cabbage

1 bunch each of fresh basil and parsley

200ml/7 fl oz cream

125g/5oz freshly grated Cheddar cheese

Pinch each of cayenne and freshly ground nutmeg

Preparation time: 50 minutes
Standing time: 1 hour
Baking time: 40 minutes
Nutritional value:
Analysis per piece, if divided into 12 slices, approx:
- 1300kJ/310kcal
- 11g protein
- 22g fat
- 16g carbohydrate

Knead the flour together with a pinch of salt, 1 egg, the cubed butter and 3 tbsps ice-cold water. Roll out to a 36cm/14in circle and line the tin with it, pressing halfway up the edge of the tin. Refrigerate for 1 hour. • Skin and dice the tomatoes, cutting out the stalk. Cut the cabbage into strips. Remove any large stalks from the herbs and chop. • Combine the tomatoes with the cabbage and herbs and spread on the pastry base. • Whisk the remaining eggs with the cream, cheese, remaining salt and the herbs and pour onto the vegetables. Bake on the centre shelf of a preheated 200°C/400°F/Gas Mark 6 oven for about 40 minutes until golden-brown.

Mushroom and Bacon Quiche
illustrated right

Quantities for 1 28cm/11in springform tin:

100g/4oz wheatmeal flour

150g/5¹/₂oz buckwheat flour

1 tsp salt • 4 eggs

125g/5oz soft butter

150g/5¹/₂oz rindless streaky bacon

1 large onion

600g/1¹/₂lbs mushrooms

1 tbsp lemon juice

1 bunch of chives

200ml/7 fl oz cream

75g/3oz freshly gratedd cheese

pinch of black pepper

Preparation time: 1 hour
Standing time: 1 hour
Baking time: 40 minutes
Nutritional value:
Analysis per piece, if divided into 12 slices, approx:
- 1510kJ/360kcal
- 11g protein
- 28g fat
- 17g carbohydrate

Knead together the flours with a pinch of salt, the egg, cubed butter and 2 tbsps ice-cold water. • Roll the dough out to a 36cm/15in circle and line the tin with it, pressing it up the edge; refrigerate for 1 hour. • Dice the bacon and chop the onion finely. Wipe and slice the mushrooms and drizzle on the lemon juice. • Fry the bacon over a moderate heat until the fat begins to run; add the onions and fry until translucent. • Chop the chives. • Combine the mushrooms with the bacon and chives and spread over the pastry base. • Whisk the remaining eggs with the cream, cheese, pepper and remaining salt and pour over the mushrooms. • Bake in a preheated 200°C/400°F/Gas Mark 6 oven for 40 minutes.

Onion Tart

A variation on the traditional Swiss onion flan

Quantities for 1 28cm/11in quiche dish:
400g/14oz strong plain flour
1 tbsp very fine soya flour
21g/³/₄oz fresh yeast or 10g/¹/₄oz dry yeast
1 tsp honey
100ml/4 fl oz lukewarm water
100g/4oz rindless streaky bacon
4 tbsps sunflower oil
500g/1lb 2oz onions
¹/₂ tsp sea salt • 4 eggs
200g/7oz sour cream
1 tsp caraway seeds
¹/₄ tsp sea salt
2 tbsps chopped chives
Butter for the quiche dish

Preparation time: 1 hour
Rising time: 45 minutes
Baking time: 50 minutes
Nutritional value:
Analysis per piece, if divided into 12 slices, approx:
- 920kJ/220kcal
- 9g protein
- 14g fat
- 15g carbohydrate

Pour the flour on a work surface and make a well in the centre. Crumble the fresh yeast into the centre and drizzle on the honey. If using dry yeast, blend the yeast with the honey. Stir in the dissolved yeast with the water and a little of the flour, cover and leave to rise for 15 minutes. • Dice the bacon and fry in the oil until crispy. • Slice the onions and fry in the bacon fat. • Knead the starter dough with the remaining flour, cover and leave to rise for 20 minutes. • Butter the quiche dish. • Knead the dough again, adding a little more water or white flour if required. • Roll out the dough and line the dish with it, cover and leave to rise for 10 minutes. • Spread the onion mixture over the base of the pastry. Whisk the eggs with the sour cream, caraway seeds and salt, pour onto the onions and bake on the centre shelf of a preheated 180°C/350°F/Gas Mark 4 oven for 50 minutes. • Sprinkle on the chopped chives and serve hot.

Vegetable Pie with Cheese Sauce

Cauliflower, broccoli, fennel and tomatoes in a light cheese and oil pastry

Quantities for 1 baking sheet:

FOR THE FILLING:

1 small cauliflower (500g/1lb 2oz)
300g/10oz broccoli
1 fennel bulb
5 tomatoes
250ml/9 fl oz stock
1 small garlic clove
150g/5½oz Cheddar cheese
50g/2oz butter
4 tbsps flour
250ml/9 fl oz milk
125g/5oz crème fraîche
Pinch each of salt, white pepper and nutmeg
4 tbsps walnuts

FOR THE PASTRY:

150g/5½oz low fat curd cheese
5 tbsps milk • 6 tbsps oil
1 egg yolk • 1 tsp salt
300g/10oz wheatmeal flour
3 tsps baking powder
Butter for the baking sheet

Preparation time: 1 hour
Baking time: 50-55 minutes
Nutritional value:

Analysis per piece, if divided into 12 slices, approx:
- 1425kJ/340kcal
- 14g protein
- 21g fat
- 27g carbohydrate

Strip the green leaves off the cauliflower and divide into individual florets. Cut the stalks off the broccoli and slice. Cut the stalk off the fennel and cut away the hard outer leaves. Finely chop the feathery green part of the fennel and set aside. Cut the fennel bulb in half and slice thinly. • Divide the tomatoes into eighths, removing the stalks. • Bring the stock to the boil and add the cauliflower florets, broccoli and fennel pieces; simmer for 10 minutes and drain, reserving the stock. • Grate the cheese. • Melt the butter and fry the crushed garlic gently. Add the flour and stir until golden; add the stock and

milk gradually. Boil the sauce for a few minutes, stirring continuously. • Stir the crème fraîche and cheese into the sauce. Season with the salt, pepper and nutmeg and add the green fennel. • Chop the walnuts. • To make the pastry, stir together the curd cheese, milk, oil, egg yolk, salt and half the flour. Combine the remaining flour with the baking powder and knead into the dough. • Butter the baking sheet. • Roll the pastry out on the baking sheet, pushing it up the edges. • Arrange the vegetables on the pastry, pour on the sauce and scatter on the nuts. • Slide the pie onto the centre shelf of the cold oven and bake at 200°C/400°F/Gas Mark 6 for 50 to 55 minutes until golden; after 40 minutes reduce the temperature to 180°C/350°F/Gas Mark 4. • Serve hot.

Our Tip: You can use any vegetables you choose, bearing in mind that their flavours should

complement each other and provide a good colour contrast.

Beetroot Quiche

Discreetly flavoured with cream and dill

Quantities for 1 28cm/11in quiche dish:
500g/1lb 2oz small beetroot
125g/5oz wheatmeal flour
125g/5oz buckwheat flour
1 egg • Pinch of salt
100g/4oz chilled butter
1 bunch of dill
100g/4oz walnuts
200g/7oz sour cream
150g/5¹/₂oz crème fraîche
3 eggs
Salt and pepper
Oil for the quiche dish

Cooking time: 1 hour
Preparation time: 45 minutes
Standing time: 1 hour
Baking time: 1 hour
Nutritional value:
Analysis per piece, if divided into 12 slices, approx:
- 1385kJ/330kcal
- 9g protein
- 23g fat
- 22g carbohydrate

Brush the beetroot under cold water. Place in a saucepan and cover with water; simmer for about 1 hour without letting it get too soft, drain and leave to cool. • Mix the flours and knead with the egg, salt and cubed butter. • Cover the dough and refrigerate for 1 hour. • Peel and dice the beetroot. • Brush the quiche dish with oil. • Roll out the pastry to a circle and line the dish with it. Prick all over with a fork and bake blind on the centre shelf of a preheated 200°C/400°F/Gas Mark 6 oven for 15 minutes. • Chop the dill and nuts. • Combine the sour cream with the crème fraîche, eggs, salt and pepper. • Scatter the dill, beetroot and nuts over the pre-baked pastry case and pour on the cream mixture. • Bake on the top shelf for 45 minutes.

Saffron Rice Quiche

A real delicacy served hot or cold with wine

Quantities for 1 28cm/11in quiche dish:
FOR THE FILLING:
250g/8oz Italian rice
45g/1¹/₂ oz butter
1 sachet powdered saffron
250ml/9 fl oz single cream
250ml/9 fl oz chicken stock
40g/1¹/₂oz green pumpkin seeds
125ml/4 fl oz white wine
1 tsp salt • ¹/₄ tsp ground nutmeg
2 eggs
FOR THE DOUGH:
50g/2oz poppy seeds
5 tbsps white wine
200g/7oz flour
1 egg yolk • ¹/₂ tsp salt
100g/4oz butter
Butter for the quiche dish

Preparation time: 45 minutes
Baking time: 30 minutes
Nutritional value:
Analysis per piece, if divided into 12 slices, approx:
- 1425kJ/340kcal
- 9g protein
- 22g fat
- 30g carbohydrate

Fry the rice in the butter. • Add the powdered saffron to 1 tbsp warm water and dissolve in the cream. • Pour the saffron cream and chicken stock onto the rice, cover and leave for 25 minutes. • Add the pumpkin seeds, wine, salt and nutmeg and leave the rice, uncovered, to absorb the liquid – stir frequently to avoid sticking. Leave the rice to cool. • Blend the poppy seeds with the wine in a liquidiser; knead with the flour, egg yolk, salt and butter to a firm shortcrust pastry. • Butter the quiche dish. • Roll out the dough and line the dish with it. Prick the pastry all over with a fork. Pour in the rice mixture and smooth flat with a fork. Beat the eggs and pour onto the rice. • Bake on the centre shelf of a preheated 200°C/400°F/Gas Mark 6 oven for about 30 minutes.

Paprika Pie à la Pipirrana

Based on a Spanish speciality

Quantities for 1 28cm/11in springform tin:

125g/5oz butter
250g/8oz wheatmeal flour
3 eggs
Pinch of salt
1 large onion
2 yellow and 2 red peppers
150g/5½oz courgettes
2 tbsps olive oil
½ tsp each of salt, black pepper and sweet paprika
Pinch of hot paprika
1 bunch of flat-leaf parsley
100g/4oz grated Cheddar cheese
Olive oil for the springform tin

Preparation time: 50 minutes
Standing time: 30 minutes
Baking time: 35-40 minutes
Nutritional value:
Analysis per piece, if divided into 12 slices, approx:
- 1005kJ/240kcal
- 9g protein
- 16g fat
- 18g carbohydrate

Roughly knead the cubed butter with the flour, 1 egg, 2 tbsps cold water and salt. Refrigerate for 30 minutes. • Chop the onions finely and deseed and dice the peppers. Grate the courgettes coarsely. • Heat the oil and fry the onions until translucent. Add the peppers and fry for a further 5 minutes, then stir in the courgettes, season with the salt and spices and leave to cool. • Brush the springform tin with oil. • Roll out the pastry and line the tin with it. Prick all over with a fork. • Roughly chop the parsley. • Beat the remaining eggs with the cheese; combine with the parsley and vegetables and pour into the tin. • Bake on the bottom shelf of a preheated 200°C/400°F/Gas Mark 6 oven for 35 to 40 minutes.

Aubergine and Ham Pie

Hearty country fare, which goes well with dry wine

Minced Beef and Vegetable Quiche

A hearty dish with a hint of the Mediterranean

Quantities for 1 26cm/11in pie:
250g/8oz wheatmeal flour
21g/³/₄oz fresh yeast or 10g/¹/₄oz dry yeast
¹/₂ tsp sugar
125ml/4 fl oz lukewarm milk
600g/1¹/₂lbs aubergines
1 tbsp salt
40g/1¹/₂oz butter • Pinch of salt
200g/7oz uncooked ham
50g/2oz stoned black olives
2 tbsps oil • 3 eggs
100ml/4 fl oz cream
Pinch each of pepper and nutmeg
8 basil leaves
Oil for the springform tin

Preparation time: 1 hour
Rising time: 1¹/₂ hours
Baking time: 45 minutes
Nutritional value:
Analysis per piece, if divided into 12 slices, approx:
• 1090kJ/260kcal
• 10g protein
• 18g fat
• 18g carbohydrate

Make a well in the centre of the flour, crumble in the fresh yeast, sprinkle on the sugar and stir in a little milk. If using dry yeast, blend with the sugar and milk and pour onto the flour. Cover and leave to froth in a warm place for 15 minutes. • Slice aubergines, sprinkle on the salt and leave for 15 minutes. • Melt butter in the remaining milk and knead with the salt, all the remaining flour and the yeast mixture. Cover and leave to rise for 45 minutes. • Cut the ham into strips and slice the olives. Drain aubergines and pat dry. • Fry aubergines in the oil; add ham and olives, fry briefly and leave to cool. • Brush the tin with oil. • Knead the dough, roll it out and line the tin with it; leave to rise for 30 minutes. • Beat the eggs with the cream and spices. • Pour the vegetables and basil onto the pastry and pour over the egg and cream mixture. • Bake in a preheated 200°C/400°F/Gas Mark 6 oven for 45 minutes.

Quantities for 1 26cm/11in springform tin:
125g/5oz wheatmeal flour
75g/3oz cornflour
125g/5oz chilled butter
1 egg yolk
Pinch each of salt and nutmeg
1 large onion • 2 tbsps olive oil
150g/5¹/₂oz minced beef
150g/5¹/₂oz each of aubergines and courgettes
1 small beef tomato
3 garlic cloves
1 tsp each of salt, black pepper and mixed herbs
1 egg white • 4 eggs
250g/8oz Greek yogurt
Olive oil for the tin

Preparation time: 1 hour
Standing time: 45 minutes
Baking time: 30 minutes
Nutritional value:
Analysis per piece, if divided into 12 slices, approx:
• 1090kJ/260kcal
• 11g protein
• 18g fat
• 17g carbohydrate

Knead the flour with the cornflour, butter, egg yolk, 3 tbsps cold water, salt and nutmeg. Chill for 45 minutes. • Chop the onions finely and fry in the oil until translucent. Brown the mince and remove from the pan. • Cut the aubergines and courgettes into 5mm/¹/₄in cubes and fry in the remaining oil for 5 minutes. Skin the tomatoes, chop them roughly and add to the vegetables. Stir in the crushed garlic, season with the salt, pepper and herbs and fry until the liquid has been absorbed. • Combine the vegetables with the minced beef and leave to cool. • Roll out the pastry; line the greased springform tin with it. • Stir the egg white, eggs and yogurt into the vegetables and pour into the pastry case; bake for 30 minutes in a preheated 200°C/400°F/Gas Mark 6 oven.

Imaginative Party Food

These striking flans make an unusual party offering

Sweetcorn and Spring Onion Flan
illustrated bottom

Quantities for 1 28cm/11in quiche dish:

200g/7oz wheatmeal flour	
100g/4oz cornmeal	
1 tsp each of baking powder and dry yeast	
125ml/4 fl oz lukewarm water	
3 tbsps lemon juice	
4 tbsps clarified butter	
1/2 tsp salt	
1/2 tsp sugar cane granules	
150g/5 1/2oz can sweetcorn	
2 bunches spring onions	
200g/7oz hard cheese	
Butter for the quiche dish	

Preparation time: 40 minutes
Rising time: 1 hour
Baking time: 30 minutes
Nutritional value:
Analysis per piece, if divided into 12 slices, approx:

- 920kJ/220kcal
- 10g protein
- 10g fat
- 21g carbohydrate

Mix the flours with the baking powder and yeast and knead with the water, lemon juice, 2 tbsps melted clarified butter, salt and sugar cane granules. Cover and leave to rise in a warm place, until it has doubled in volume – this will take about an hour. • Butter the quiche dish. • Knead the dough again, incorporating the sweetcorn. Roll it out into a circle and line the dish with it. • Trim the spring onions and fry in the remaining clarified butter, stirring frequently, for 4 minutes. Cut them in half lengthwise and scatter on the pastry base. • Cut the ham and cheese into strips and arrange among the onions. • Bake on the bottom shelf of a preheated 200°C/400°F/Gas Mark 6 oven for 30 minutes.

Layered Cheese Flan
illustrated top

Quantities for 1 26cm/11in springform tin:

250g/8oz soft butter	
100g/4oz freshly grated Parmesan cheese	
4 eggs	
350g/11oz wheatmeal flour	
1/2 tsp each of salt and sweet paprika	
2 tsps baking powder	
250g/8oz herby cream cheese	
250g/8oz Mascarpone	
1 bunch of chives	
Butter for the tin	

Preparation time: 2 hours
Nutritional value:
Analysis per piece, if divided into 12 slices, approx:

- 2010kJ/480kcal
- 15g protein
- 37g fat
- 21g carbohydrate

Butter the springform tin. • Knead the butter and cheese together, incorporating the eggs gradually. Combine the flour with the salt, paprika and baking powder and mix into the egg and cheese mixture. • Divide the dough into 5 portions and press each one down flat onto the base of the springform tin. Bake each one on the centre shelf of a preheated 200°C/400°F/Gas Mark 6 oven for about 7 minutes until golden. • Leave each pre-baked pastry case to cool. • Mix the herby cream cheese with the Mascarpone. Spread the pastry cases with the mixture and lay one on top of the other. • Spread the remaining cheese mixture round the sides and over the top of the flan. • Chop the chives and sprinkle on the top.

Smoked Salmon Quiche

A real delicacy for those special guests – it can be served hot or cold

Quantities for 1 26cm/11in springform tin:
200g/7oz wheatmeal flour
150g/5oz butter
1 egg
2 tbsps milk
Pinch of salt
300g/10oz thinly sliced smoked salmon
750g/1lb 11oz leeks
4 eggs
6 tbsps crème fraîche
1/2 tsp each of salt and freshly ground white pepper
Pinch of nutmeg
1 tsp lemon juice
Butter for the tin

Preparation time: 40 minutes
Standing time: 30 minutes
Baking time: 30-35 minutes
Nutritional value:
Analysis per piece, if divided into 12 slices, approx:
• 1385kJ/330kcal
• 14g protein
• 18g fat
• 15g carbohydrate

Knead the flour, 100g/4 oz of the butter, the egg, milk and salt together to form an elastic dough. Wrap it in aluminium foil and refrigerate for 30 minutes. • Cut the smoked salmon into strips. • Trim the leeks and cut into broad rings. Fry gently in the rest of the butter for 6 minutes. Remove from the heat and leave to cool. • Beat the eggs with the crème fraîche, stir in the leeks and salmon and season with the salt, pepper, nutmeg and lemon juice. • Butter the springform tin. • Roll the dough out in a circle and line the tin with it, pushing it up slightly at the sides. Pour the filling over the dough. • Bake in a preheated 200°C/400°F/Gas Mark 6 oven for 30 to 35 minutes until golden.

Spring Green Quiche

Delicious hot or cold

Quantities for 1 26cm/11in springform tin:
150g/5½oz wheatmeal flour
150g/5oz butter
150g/5½oz low fat curd cheese
Pinch of salt
750g/1lb 11oz Swiss chard, turnip tops or spring greens
2 shallots
200g/7oz peeled, cooked prawns
1/2 tsp each of salt and freshly ground white pepper
Pinch of nutmeg
1/2 tsp grated lemon rind
A little lemon juice
125ml/4 fl oz cream
3 eggs
3 tbsps grated Parmesan cheese
Butter for the tin

Preparation time: 40 minutes
Standing time: 30 minutes
Baking time: 35 minutes
Nutritional value:
analysis per piece, if divided into 12 slices, approx:
• 840kJ/200kcal
• 8g protein
• 14g fat
• 11g carbohydrate

Knead the flour with 100g/4oz of the butter, the curd cheese and salt into a dough. Cover and refrigerate for 30 minutes. • Trim the leaves from the stalks of the greens, and cut the leaves into 1cm/½in strips. Blanch in boiling salted water for 5 seconds, plunge into cold water and leave to drain. Blanch the stalks for 1 minute. • Chop the shallots and fry in the rest of the butter until translucent. Add the stalks and fry for 3 minutes; combine with the prawns and leaves, and season with the salt and spices. • Butter a springform tin. Roll out the dough and line the tin with it, making a 4cm/2in high rim. Bake blind for 10 minutes in a preheated 200°C/400°F/Gas Mark 6 oven. • Beat the eggs with the cream and Parmesan. Pour the filling over the pastry case, then add the egg-and-cream mixture. • Bake for 35 minutes.

Oyster Mushroom Quiche

This quiche is at its best served straight from the oven

Quantities for 1 26cm/11in springform tin:

250g/8oz wheatmeal flour
125g/5oz butter
1 egg
Pinch of salt
1 onion
600g/1¹/₂lbs oyster mushrooms
2 tbsps olive oil
200g/7oz cooked ham
2 bunches of chives
¹/₂ tsp each of salt and freshly ground black pepper
Pinch each of freshly grated nutmeg and cayenne
¹/₂ tsp dried oregano
3 eggs
150g/5¹/₂oz crème fraîche
100g/4oz freshly grated Cheddar cheese
Butter for the tin

Preparation time: 1 hour
Standing time: 30 minutes
Baking time: 40 minutes
Nutritional value:

Analysis per piece, if divided into 12 slices, approx:

- 1340kJ/320kcal
- 14g protein
- 23g fat
- 16g carbohydrate

Knead the flour, butter, egg and salt together to form an elastic dough; refrigerate for 30 minutes. • Chop the onions finely. • Wipe the mushrooms and slice thinly. • Fry the onions in the oil until translucent, add the mushrooms and fry for 8 minutes; leave to cool. • Cut the ham into strips and add to the mushrooms. Finely chop the chives and reserve 2 tbsps of them. Add the rest to the mushrooms and season with the salt and spices. • Beat the eggs with the crème fraîche and cheese. • Grease the springform tin with butter. • Roll out the dough and line the tin with it, bringing the sides up 3cm/1in high. • Arrange the mushrooms on the dough base, add the egg-and-cream mixture and bake in a preheated 200°C/400°F/Gas Mark 6 oven for 40 minutes. Serve garnished with the remaining chives.

Patchwork Pizza

Fun to cook, fun to eat – each portion offers a different taste

Quantities for 1 baking sheet:
400g/14 oz wheatmeal flour
25g/1oz fresh yeast or 12g/¹/₂oz dry yeast
¹/₂ tsp sugar
125ml/4 fl oz lukewarm water
1 egg
1 tbsp oil
1 tsp salt
4 tbsps tomato purée
2 tsps dried oregano
1 tbsp oil
¹/₂ tsp salt
Pinch of freshly ground black pepper
2 yellow and 2 green peppers
4 tomatoes
100g/4oz black olives
200g/7oz mushrooms
16 anchovy fillets
100g/4oz freshly grated Emmental cheese
4 tbsps olive oil
Olive oil for the baking sheet

Preparation time: 1¹/₂ hours
Rising time: 1¹/₄ hours
Baking time: 35 minutes
Nutritional value:
 analysis per piece, if divided into 16 slices, approx:
- 920kJ/220kcal
- 11g protein
- 10g fat
- 21g carbohydrate

Pour the flour into a bowl and make a well in the centre. Crumble in the fresh yeast and mix with the sugar, a little water and a little flour. If using dry yeast, blend the yeast with the sugar and water and pour onto the flour. Cover and leave to rise in a warm place for 20 minutes. • Knead the starter dough together with the remaining flour and water, the egg, the oil and the salt until it forms a smooth, elastic dough which leaves the bowl clean. Cover and leave to rise until it has doubled in volume – this will take about 45 minutes. • Combine the tomato purée with the oregano, oil, salt and pepper. • Deseed the peppers and cut into 1cm/¹/₂in strips. Skin and chop the tomatoes. Halve and stone the olives. Wipe and slice the mushrooms. Cut the anchovy fillets in half lengthwise. • Brush the baking sheet with oil. • Roll the dough out on the baking sheet and push up the sides to form an edge. Cover and leave to rise for a further 10 to 15 minutes. • Spread the tomato purée on the dough base and mark out 16 oblongs with a knife. • On each oblong arrange 2 anchovy fillets in a crisscross pattern and pour 1 of the vegetable mixtures on top. • Scatter the olives and cheese all over the pizza and drizzle on the olive oil. • Bake on the centre shelf of a preheated 200°C/400°F/Gas Mark 6 oven for about 35 minutes until golden. Serve piping hot.

Our Tip: You can use other combinations of vegetables, such as sliced courgettes with shallots and garlic, mushrooms mixed with chopped parsley or sweetcorn combined with diced red pepper. The anchovies can be omitted.

Mediterranean Quiches

These are both served hot and small portions make a tasty starter

Camembert Quiche
illustrated left

Quantities for 1 26cm/11in springform tin:

200g/7oz wheatmeal flour
75g/3oz butter • 1 egg yolk
2 tbsps milk • ½ tsp salt
250g/8oz Camembert
5 eggs
150g/5½oz crème fraîche
1 tsp mixed herbs
1 tsp freshly ground black pepper
Butter for the tin

Preparation time: 40 minutes
Standing time: 30 minutes
Baking time: 40 minutes
Nutritional value:
Analysis per piece, if divided into 12 slices, approx:
- 1300kJ/310kcal
- 13g protein
- 23g fat
- 13g carbohydrate

Knead the flour, butter, egg yolk, milk and salt together to form shortcrust pastry and refrigerate for 30 minutes. • Derind the Camembert and cut into 5mm/¼in slices. Beat the eggs with the crème fraîche and season well with the herbs and pepper. • Butter the springform tin. • Roll out the dough and line the tin with it, pushing it up the sides to form a raised edge. • Arrange the pieces of cheese on the pastry case and pour on the eggs and cream mixture. Bake on the centre shelf of a preheated 200°C/400°F/Gas Mark 6 oven for 40 minutes.

Olive Pie
illustrated right

Quantities for 1 26cm/11in pie:

450g/1lb frozen puff pastry
250g/8oz mushrooms
120g/4½oz carrots
2 spring onions
50g/2oz clarified butter
600g/1½lbs minced beef
100g/4oz stuffed green olives
100g/4oz crème fraîche
50g/2oz grated Cheddar cheese
½ tsp each of salt and freshly ground black pepper
Pinch of cayenne
½ tsp each of dried oregano and thyme
1 egg yolk

Preparation time: 1 hour
Baking time: 1 hour
Nutritional value:
Analysis per piece, if divided into 12 slices, approx:
- 1510kJ/360kcal
- 16g protein
- 28g fat
- 14g carbohydrate

Defrost the puff dough at room temperature. • Wipe and slice the mushrooms. • Scrape and grate the carrots. • Chop the spring onions. • Heat the clarified butter and fry the mushrooms, carrots and onions for 8 minutes. Remove from the pan. • Fry the mince in the remaining fat, breaking it up with the spatula, and add to the vegetables. Stir the olives, crème fraîche and cheese into the filling and season well with the salt and spices. • Roll out two-thirds of the pastry to the size of the springform tin; line the tin with the pastry, pushing it up at the sides to form a 4cm/2in high rim. • Pour the filling over the pastry case. • Roll out the remaining dough to a circle a little larger than the springform tin and cut a small hole in the centre. • Lay the pastry lid on top of the filling and press the edges together. • Brush the pastry lid with the beaten egg yolk and bake in a preheated 200°C/400°F/Gas Mark 6 oven for 1 hour or until golden.

Ratatouille Quiche

A very special quiche, with a rich cream filling

Quantities for 1 28cm/11in springform tin:

FOR THE RATATOUILLE:

350g/11oz aubergines

500g/1lb 2oz courgettes

250g/8oz onions

2 red and 2 green peppers

4 garlic cloves

500g/1 lb 2oz beefsteak tomatoes

6 tbsps olive oil

1 tsp each of salt and freshly ground white pepper

1 bunch each of basil and parsley

FOR THE SHORTCRUST DOUGH:

250g/8oz wheatmeal flour

$^1/_2$ tsp salt

125g/5oz chilled butter

1 egg yolk

FOR THE FILLING:

125ml/4 fl oz each of cream and crème fraîche

2 eggs

150g/5$^1/_2$oz freshly grated Gruyère cheese

Butter for the tin

Preparation time: 1 hour
Standing time: 1 hour
Baking time: 45 minutes
Nutritional value:

Analysis per piece, if divided into 12 slices, approx:

• 1760kJ/420kcal
• 12g protein
• 31g fat
• 22g carbohydrate

Cut the aubergines into 2cm/1in cubes and the courgettes into 1cm/$^1/_2$in slices. Slice the onions in rings. Deseed the peppers and cut into equal-sized narrow strips. Finely chop the garlic. Skin and quarter the tomatoes. • Heat the oil in a casserole and fry the onion rings until lightly browned; add the pepper strips and garlic and fry for 2 minutes, stirring frequently. Add the remaining vegetables, salt and pepper. Cover and simmer over a low heat for 20 minutes. • Chop the herbs. • To make the dough, mix the flour with the salt, tip it onto a work surface and make a well in the centre. • Add the cubed butter to the edge of the flour. Put the egg yolk and 2 tbsps of ice-cold water into the well and knead it quickly to form a smooth, elastic dough. Wrap in aluminium foil and refrigerate for 1 hour. • Cool the vegetables and leave to drain in a sieve. Mix in the chopped herbs. • Whisk the cream with the crème fraîche, eggs and cheese and stir into the ratatouille. • Butter the springform tin. • Roll out the pastry on a lightly floured work surface into a circle slightly larger than the springform tin and line the tin with it, raising the sides to form a 5cm/2in high rim. Pour in the ratatouille and bake the quiche on the centre shelf of a preheated 200°C/400°F/Gas Mark 6 oven for 45 minutes. • Serve hot.

Our Tip: As an alternative, try using organic wholewheat flour for the pastry.

Essential Ingredients for Baking

Grain and grain products have formed the basis of healthy nutrition for centuries – it is only the way they are prepared which has altered over the years. In the beginning, people mixed a paste from ground barley and wheat and water. Sourdough made from the yeasts in the air were added and the round, flat breads were baked on hot stones. There are scenes of baking in the Egyptian pyramids. The art of bread baking was refined in the Middle Ages. Today bread constitutes a major element of our diet. Quite apart from the health aspect, the fragrance and taste of home-baked bread are not to be missed.

Refined Flours

After the Industrial Revolution, and the move away from the country to the town, it became necessary to find a way to make flour keep for longer. This entailed discovering how to remove the bran and wheatgerm from the grain during the grinding process. This resulted in fine, white, refined flours, consisting purely of the endosperm, from which not only the bran and germ, but also essential, health-giving ingredients such as vitamins, minerals and trace elements were missing.

Buying and Storing Grain

When baking wholewheat bread, it is advisable to use only freshly-ground flour whenever possible. Grain itself has natural 'keeping qualities'. In a dry place at room temperature it will stay fresh for years, stored in jute or linen sacks or in an open box. Oats should not be stored for longer than one year. Organic flour can be purchased in health food shops. There should be no evidence of dirt or foreign seed particles, or the somewhat larger and clearly visible blackish specks of ergot which is more commonly found in rye. Ergot is a potent fungal poison. If you buy newly harvested grain direct from the grower, you should make sure that it has had a sufficiently lengthy drying period; if possible it should not be stored before mid November. Dry grain freezes well. Do not buy ground flour until you need it.

Types of Grain and Other Ingredients

Wheat

This is the most significant bread grain, being ideally suited to baking thanks to its high gluten content. Gluten allows the flour to rise well when mixed with yeast by holding in the carbon dioxide which develops as the yeast 'digests' the flour, the result being light bread. Wheat is easily digestible and has a high vitamin B1 content.

Rye

Nutritionally, rye is very similar to wheat, but has a lower gluten content. Yeast is not an adequate raising agent for rye flour or coarsely-ground grain – sour dough, a leaven or baking powder is required. Rye flour is often mixed with wheatmeal flour to make a lighter bread. Rye is easier to grow than wheat in cooler, northern climes and even in mountainous regions.

Buckwheat

These are the seeds of the knotgrass plant, which are used like grain. The question of organic farming does not arise as buckwheat will not grow in chemically fertilised soil. Buckwheat is easily digestible; buckwheat groats (sometimes also known as kasha) are better value than ready ground flour and good for fine grinding.

wheat

rye

oats

millet

green spelt

wholewheat flour

coarse oatmeal

barley

fresh yeast

dried yeast

baking powder

buckwheat flour

buckwheat

Barley

Being rich in vitamins and easily digestible, barley is well known as a cure for stomach, intestinal and liver complaints. It is not ideal for bread baking as it has practically no gluten content, although it was the first grain used for such a purpose. Small quantities are combined with other types of flour, as pure barley breads dry out quickly.

Oats

Of all the types of grain, oats are richest in fat and protein. They also contain 25 percent more Vitamin B1 than wheat. They are only used for bread baking in combination with wheat because they lack a specific type of protein. The slightly nutty aroma of oat grains is enhanced by roasting and this gives the bread a strong, delicious flavour.

Oatmeal

These are oat grains which have been steamed and kiln-dried, then rolled into flakes. The whole grain is pressed to make coarse oatmeal; fine oatmeal is the product of the ground grain. Oatmeal can be kneaded into the dough during bread making or sprinkled over the shaped loaf.

Millet

This grain, best known in Britain as bird seed, is richest in minerals and has a particularly high silicic acid content. It also contains many fat-soluble vitamins, protein and trace elements, and is easily digestible. The small, golden-yellow grain is easily grown and flourishes even in a drought; in Africa it is still a staple food. It was once an essential component of wedding banquets in central Europe, where it symbolised fertility and prosperity. It is only used in bread making when combined with other flours, as it contains no gluten, but it does round off the flavour of the bread and makes it more crusty.

Corn (Maize)

Corn (maize) is the largest of all the grains and comes from Peru and Mexico, where it was first cultivated by the natives. No other grain has such varied uses. It is used as the basis for American whiskey and salad oil, as a vegetable (both fresh and canned) and as animal feed. It contains no gluten and must therefore be combined with other flours for bread baking. It is not suitable for yeast doughs and is best used for cakes, combined with baking powder. Only whole cornmeal contains the germ. Cornmeal (also known as polenta) comes from the grain from which the germ has been removed and is then ground finely or coarsely. Cornflour, the very finely ground refined flour from maize, was originally developed as a stiffening starch used in the clothing industry, which was patented as a food by Brown and Polson of Paisley, Scotland, in 1884.

Brown rice

As with most grains, the most valuable elements of the rice grain are found in the bran and germ; thus it is advisable to eat only wholegrain and unpolished brown rice. Rice flour is added to bread dough in small quantities. Dietetic unleavened breads are baked from pure rice flour.

Soya beans

Soya beans are heat treated before grinding into very fine, golden-yellow soya flour; this treatment kills off any undesirable bacteria. If you are making your own soya flour, you should always roast the beans before grinding them. Soya flour does not contain any binding elements and is therefore added to other types of flour. It keeps the bread fresh for longer, makes it easier to cut and improves both flavour and texture. It is also used in the food industry.

Yeast

Yeast is a completely natural, biological raising agent. It is a type of fungus which is cultivated for use in bread making. Sour dough is made of yeasts which occur naturally in the air, which may be one of a number of strains. Yeast works by causing enzymes to break down the sugar present in the flour into carbon dioxide and alcohol; this process can be seen in the frothing and bubbling which occurs as the yeast begins to work. Fresh yeast is sold in small blocks weighing about 42g/1¹/₂oz cubes; dried yeast comes in 7g/1/8oz sachets. You should abide by the sell-by date in both cases. Fresh yeast should be light greyish-

olive oil

Parmesan cheese

wholemeal rye flour

heat extraction flour

cornmeal

coarsely-ground soya

Emmental cheese

liquid sour dough

cornflour

sour dough extract

brown rice

soya beans

starter or leaven

soya flour

Spices Used in Breadmaking

brown in colour, with no dark areas, smooth and malleable and with no dry, cracked patches. It will stay fresh for one week if kept in the refrigerator, after which time it will have lost some of its raising quality. Dried yeast has been vacuum dried at 60°C/140°F and only becomes 'live' again in the dough. It can be kept for 6 to 12 months. There are now varieties of yeast on the market which should not be mixed with liquid first, but incorporated directly into the flour. Always follow the manufacturers' instructions on the packet, in preference to the recipe instructions, where there is a conflict.

Sourdough

This raising agent is particularly suited to baking dark breads, such as rye bread. You can buy natural sour dough, produced without preservatives, at your baker or health food shop; some well-stocked supermarkets even sell it. Sour dough extract can be purchased as granules or powder in 15g/1/2oz packs. You should abide by the sell-by date for both. Sour dough extract is useful as a 'starter' for making your own sour dough.

Baking powder

Baking powder is a chemical raising agent which produces carbon dioxide during the baking process. Used sparingly, it has the same effect as yeast in lightening the dough and making it digestible. Too high a proportion used in a recipe will impart an unpleasant flavour to the dough or batter.

Olive oil

Olive oil is often used for the preparation of pizzas and rich cakes and breads. It is advisable to buy it in small quantities as the valuable cold-pressed, unrefined oils quickly go rancid. It should be stored in the refrigerator if possible.

Parmesan cheese

This is a tangy Italian hard cheese made from semi-skimmed cow's milk, which is popular as a topping and for tangy fillings. It is best freshly grated as it dries out quickly, losing its delicate aroma.

Cheddar or Emmental cheese

These yellow cheeses, or those of similar consistency, can be grated coarsely or finely. They are often kneaded into a yeast or shortcrust pastry dough or added to vegetable and meat fillings. They can also be sprinkled on loaves before they are placed in the oven or, combined with cream and eggs, poured over a pastry base to make a golden cheese filling for a tart or quiche. Most yellow cheeses are full fat and thus rich in calories, but calorie-reduced yellow cheeses are available.

Sea salt

Sea salt contains more minerals such as iodine, magnesium and calcium than normal cooking salt. It is added to yeast dough to control the rising process. Though salt increases the length of time bread stays fresh and improves the texture, it should be used sparingly for health reasons. Coarse salt is often sprinkled on rolls and pretzels.

Spices Used in Bread-Baking

Aniseed

This has been used in baking for thousands of years. The aniseed plant's seeds have a bitter-sweet tang; if possible they should be used fresh, either ground or crushed with a pestle and mortar, because they quickly lose their flavour. Aniseed is often used in medicine and in the manufacture of liqueurs and spirits.

Fennel

Fennel contains an appetizing, volatile oil which has the added benefit of preventing flatulence. The seeds are a natural cough medicine and their slightly sweet taste, whether used whole or ground, is much prized in bread baking. They are at their best when ground together with the grains just prior to baking. Fennel is quite strong and should therefore be used sparingly.

golden syrup

caraway seeds

honey

hulled pumpkin seeds

unhulled sesame seed

cardamom

coriander

unhulled pumpkin seeds

fennel

Caraway seeds

These have the same medicinal qualities as fennel. They are also the perfect complement to dark breads and help to round off the flavour, as well as improving digestibility. Caraway seeds should also be freshly ground if possible.

Coriander

Combined with aniseed, fennel and caraway seeds, coriander is the ideal bread spice. The grains have a powerful, slightly sweet taste and can be used both whole and ground.

Sesame seeds

These are the light, oily seeds of the sesame plant. You can buy hulled and unhulled sesame seeds; the unhulled variety are usually used for bread making. The seeds are either kneaded into the dough, or you can coat the whole shaped loaf with them before baking. Their nutty flavour is enhanced by being briefly dry fried.

Sunflower seeds

These highly nutritious seeds can be kneaded into the dough, either coarsely chopped or whole, or sprinkled onto the shaped loaf. They have a high oil content and are therefore fairly rich in calories. They increase the protein and mineral content of the bread. As with nuts, they should not be stored for too long as they do become rancid.

Pumpkin seeds

Like sunflower seeds, pumpkin seeds contain valuable oil, protein and minerals. They soften during baking and can therefore be kneaded whole into the dough.

Poppyseeds

Poppyseeds are rich in oil. In central Europe, they are usually ground and combined with milk to make a sweet fillings for cakes or pastries. They are best freshly ground in a spice grinder or coffee grinder. Whole poppy seeds make a delicious topping for rolls and breads.

Pistachio nuts

These tasty green nuts come from the Near and Middle East and are now also grown in the United States. They have a high oil content and quickly become rancid; if they are stored for a long time they will lose their attractive green colour. They add a spicy flavour to breads and pastries.

Seville oranges

Seville or bitter oranges are usually used for making marmalade, liqueurs and refreshing citrus drinks; they are too bitter to be eaten raw. The rind is used for candied orange peel but can be used in baking if finely grated. However, bitter oranges are only in season for a limited time. Untreated lemon rind is also used in bread making.

full cream milk

buttermilk

kefir

yogurt

cream cheese

low fat curd cheese

pistachios

pistachio kernels

lemons

hulled sesame seeds

hulled sunflower seeds

poppy seeds

Baking Tins and Kitchen Equipment

Milk and Dairy Products

Milk

Milk aids the fermentation process, making bread light and soft. Full cream milk should be used for baking.

Buttermilk

This is the liquid which is left over once cream has been turned into butter. It is low in fat but otherwise has the same nutrients and active ingredients as milk, such as protein, calcium, potassium and vitamins. Up to 10 percent water and up to 15 percent skimmed milk or skimmed milk powder can be added to buttermilk. Pure buttermilk contains no additives and has a better flavour. It lightens the bread dough and imparts a delicate flavour.

Yogurt

Yogurt can also be added to dough. Greek style yogurt has a fat content of 10 percent, full-fat yogurt at least 3.5 percent and low-fat yogurt 1.5 percent.

Kefir

Kefir is thick, soured milk. It is available with the same fat content as milk and as full cream kefir, with 10 percent fat content.

Curd Cheese and Cream Cheese

Doughs made from a combination of curd cheese and oil or butter are easy to prepare and guarantee a light result, with a slightly sharp tang. Curd cheese lightens a yeast dough too. Low fat curd cheese, also known as low fat soft cheese, is ideally suited to baking and offers the largest proportion of valuable milk protein. Cream cheese has a creamier consistency and is used to fill savoury flans and quiches.

Baking Tins and Kitchen Equipment

Country people relied on home baked bread long after urban households had begin relying on their local baker to provide all the bread they needed. In the past, the housewife would have devoted one or two days a month to bread baking. Many farms had a special outside oven or bakehouse.

These days, home baking is increasing in popularity all over the country. People are finding that they enjoy preparing not only elaborate cakes and attractive pastries for special occasions, but even the family's daily bread. The fragrant aroma of home baked bread can be just as impressive as a cleverly devised menu. The preparations required for bread baking are simple. All you need to start are time and patience, a few interesting recipes, strong hands to knead and shape the dough and an oven with a properly calibrated thermostat, even heat distribution and removable racks. Many modern households have gadgets to make things even easier; for kneading heavy dough, for example, you can use an electric hand mixer or the dough hook or blades of a food processor.

The following notes on baking tins and other equipment which make bread baking even easier have been designed just as much for those who would like to become more adventurous after a few successful attempts, as for the serious wholegrain bread baker.

Different Types of Baking Tin

It is safest to use loaf tins for baking, because a dough which is too loose or has been left to rise for too long will not have the chance to over expand. The range of loaf tins now available is enormous, so your choice rather depends on the extent of your bread baking, whether you simply bake bread now and again for pleasure or regularly supply your family with home baked bread, whether you bake in advance and freeze it or consume the loaf immediately. The size of your oven should also be taken into account. The various shapes of cake tin and springform tin to be found in most kitchens can also be used for bread baking, as can glazed and unglazed earthenware pots (bricks), flowerpots, heavy cast-iron pots and roasting bags.

Loaf tins are usually 20, 25, 30 or 35cm (8, 10, 12 or 14in) long and slightly wider than cake tins. An oblong tin divided into four separate sections allows you to bake four small breads from one batch of dough. A range of brioche tins in various sizes make a delightful gift to those who love

normal loaf tins

extra-wide loaf tins

unglazed earthenware pot

round loaf tin

loaf tins for
small breads

spatula

oven thermometer

brioche tin

these rich French breads. Round and oblong loaf tins are available in various materials, including tinplate, aluminium, Pyrex, china and clay. Loaf and cake tins are available with non-stick surfaces, of which silverstone is the most lasting.

Useful Equipment

If you are fond of baking cakes, you will already have most of the equipment required for bread baking, for example, a palette knife, wooden, metal and plastic spatulas and different sized mixing bowls, measuring jugs, wooden spoons, pastry brushes and a wire rack for cooling the loaf, kitchen scissors and a toaster. High-grade steel mixing bowls are advisable for bread baking as they absorb heat well while the dough is rising. Sour dough should not be allowed to ferment in a plastic bowl. A rolling pin with a removable

handle is useful for when the dough has to be rolled out directly on a greased baking sheet. Checking the oven temperature with an oven thermometer, available in most hardware shops, can be useful since the oven temperature has a considerable influence on the success (or otherwise) of your bread baking, and temperatures sometimes differ from those displayed on the oven's own gauge. Kneading heavy yeast and sour doughs by hand is tiring; electric hand mixers with a dough hook, and food processors do save much of the work. Some food processors also have a grinding attachment which can be used for grain or seeds.

If you want to bake dark breads that have the typical grooves of a bread basket, you will need an oblong or circular cane basket. Leave the dough to prove in the basket before placing it on a baking tray and baking.

Buying Home Milling Equipment

Many people now grind their own coffee beans and even spices because of the tempting aromas in the kitchen, and to ensure freshness. Some people, who are doing a large amount of wholewheat baking, are even going so far as to grind their own flour. This ensures that no valuable elements are lost. It is a little-known fact that the most nutritious constituents and the flavour of the flour start to evaporate even a few hours after grinding.

If you do not want to go to the expense of purchasing a flour mill, you can use a grinding attachment on a food processor for small quantities.

For the beginner, there are small, hand-held flour mills which can be acquired relatively cheaply. If you are planning to bake bread frequently, an electric mill is best. The grinding mechanism can be made of flint, high-grade steel or ceramic. Although fairly coarse flour is suitable for most breads, your mill should also be able to grind flour finely, so that you can

make delicate pastries or wholewheat pasta if necessary. If you can find a shop which will give you a demonstration of the flour mill, your decision will be easier to make. Manufacturers' instructions will give you precise technical details and information on other mills which the shop may not have in stock.

hand-held flour mill

bread baskets

toaster

electric hand mixer

rolling pin

mixing bowls

measuring jug

wooden spoon

pastry brushes

kitchen scissors

knife

wire rack

125

Index

Index